WINSTON
CHURCHILL

WINSTON CHURCHILL

SOLDIER, STATESMAN, ARTIST

BY JOHN B. SEVERANCE

CLARION BOOKS ◆ NEW YORK

The lion decoration on each of the chapter openings
is adapted from the Churchill family coat of arms.

FRONTISPIECE: Churchill as the new Under-Secretary of State
at the Colonial Office, at the age of thirty-one, in 1905.

CLARION BOOKS
a Houghton Mifflin Company imprint
215 Park Avenue South, New York, NY 10003
Text copyright © 1996 by John B. Severance

For information about this and other Houghton Mifflin trade and reference books and multimedia products,
visit The Bookstore at Houghton Mifflin on the World Wide Web at (http://www.hmco.com/trade/).

Book design by Sylvia Frezzolini Severance
Type is 12.25 point New Baskerville.
Printed in the USA

LIBRARY OF CONGRESS CATALOGING-IN-PUBLICATION DATA
Severance, John B.
Winston Churchill: soldier, statesman, artist / John B. Severance.
p.   cm.   Includes bibliographical references (pp. 134-136) and index.
ISBN 0-395-69853-7
1. Churchill, Winston, Sir, 1874-1965—Juvenile literature. 2. Prime ministers—Great Britain—
Biography—Juvenile literature. 3. Great Britain—History—20th century—Juvenile literature.
[1. Churchill, Winston, Sir, 1874-1965. 2. Prime ministers.] I. Title.
DA566.9.C5S43 1996   94-25129
941.084'092—dc20   CIP
[B]   AC
HOR 10 9 8 7 6 5 4 3 2 1

To Sylvia
for her loving collaboration.

———————◆———————

CONTENTS

Churchill portraits: A bronze bust of Winston in later life, displayed in front of a photograph of him taken in 1899.

CHAPTER I

MEASURING THE MAN

WINSTON CHURCHILL WAS ONCE ASKED what was the most important skill for a person who wanted to go into politics. "It is the ability to foretell what is going to happen tomorrow, next week, next month, and next year," he said. "And to have the ability afterwards to explain why it didn't happen."

Churchill had great foresight, but he knew the future is mostly unpredictable. He himself was unpredictable. He changed political parties twice during his half-century in public life. Such a varied career meant that many people saw Winston in many different ways. Was he a man of peace? Was he a man of war? Did he use the political stage to satisfy his own enormous ego? Even his enemies said he had tremendous strength and energy. Churchill was colorful.

Churchill was a lonely child whose parents paid very little attention to him. Perhaps loneliness made him imaginative. Imagination can lead to adventure. In his childhood, in his army experiences, as a journalist, and even as a politician, he always went out of his way to be where the activity was the most exciting.

His taste for dramatic adventure sometimes got him into trouble. He was criticized for his escapades in 1899 during the Boer War in South Africa. His calls for military preparedness in 1912 and 1913 before World War I, and again in 1937 and 1938 before World War II, caused some people to say Churchill was a warmonger. A number of his opponents made the same claim in 1946 after his famous anticommunist "Iron Curtain" speech in Fulton, Missouri. But he felt strong action was the only way governments could help their people. He believed in fighting a hundred percent for right. He also believed in showing generosity to the vanquished. He was not afraid to speak his mind even if no one agreed with him. He was courageous.

Being unpopular didn't bother Churchill if he was sure he was right. He took great pains to dig out all the facts to inform himself before he decided what was right. He often discovered important facts that other people did not know or did not care to know. He would study these facts and find ways to present them to the public even when no one wanted to listen. He was tenacious.

Lots of people have imagination, courage, and tenacity. Few people have them in the amount or combination that Churchill did. Even fewer are able to express these qualities in the magnificent language that he could command, either in writing essays and books, or in speaking to Parliament and the British nation. Winston Churchill chose words for their resonant sounds and arranged them in sentences with rolling rhythms that inspired millions of people and settled in the memory of history. Queen Victoria was ruling the British Empire when he joined the army in 1895, and he was elected to Parliament in 1900, the year before she died. He went on to serve in government under four kings and resigned as Prime Minister of Great Britain in 1955 during the fourth year of the reign of Queen Elizabeth II. This child of the nineteenth century played major roles as a man of the twentieth.

Four of the six monarchs Churchill served: Standing behind Queen Victoria (left to right) are her grandson, the future King George V, and her son, the future Edward VII. The little boy beside the Queen is the future King Edward VIII, uncle of Queen Elizabeth II.

Top: Winston's parents, Lord Randolph Churchill and his wife,
Lady Randolph Churchill, the former Jennie Jerome of New York.
Bottom: Winston at the age of seven.

CHAPTER II

EARLY ADVENTURES

Less than a hundred years before he was born, some of Winston Churchill's ancestors were in George Washington's army, fighting British redcoats in the American Revolution. One of his great-great-grandmothers was an Iroquois Indian named Mehitabel Beach. His mother, Jennie Jerome, was born in Brooklyn and her father, Leonard Jerome, was a flamboyant and wealthy New Yorker who owned and edited *The New York Times*. Churchill was half American. Nevertheless, his growing up was very British and very aristocratic. His father, Lord Randolph Churchill, was descended from the dukes of Marlborough and had grown up in the vast and elegant atmosphere of Blenheim Palace, the family home in central England since 1710. Winston was born there on November 30, 1874.

All during his childhood, Churchill was mostly ignored by his parents. His mother had an extravagant social life and his father was very much involved in government. As an adult Winston wrote of his mother, "She shone for me like the evening star, I loved her dearly but at a distance." He wished Lord Randolph had run a grocery store. "I should have got to know my father better, which would have been a great joy to me." Winston was closer to his nanny, Mrs. Anne Everest, than he was to his own parents. He kept in touch with "Woomany" long after she left the Churchill household. He was with her when she died in the summer of 1895 and he made the arrangements for her funeral.

Winston's earliest memories were of the family living on a large estate in Ireland. He was quite happy there until Mrs. Everest tried to prepare him for lessons with a governess or tutor. When the governess arrived, he hid in the bushes for hours. But the lessons got started and Winston did not like any of them, especially arithmetic. "If it was not right it was wrong," he wrote many years later in his autobiography. "It was not any use being 'nearly right.'" And it was very confusing when the numbers "got into debt with one another: you had to borrow one or carry one, and afterwards you had to pay back the one you had borrowed." Winston worried that he would not have time to play with his toy soldiers or ramble in the gardens. He did not realize that he would be leaving those gardens behind soon after the birth of his baby brother, Jack.

Like most upper-class little boys in Victorian England, Winston was sent away to boarding school when he was only seven years old. The school his parents chose was fashionable, expensive, and very strict. Boys were punished by being flogged until they bled and other boys could hear the screams. "How I hated this school," wrote Winston. "I counted the days and hours to the end of every term." After two years he became so sick he was transferred to a gentler

Left to right: Winston's brother Jack, their mother Jennie, and Winston at fifteen.

school. "At this school I was allowed to learn things that interested me." About this time Winston's father gave him a copy of *Treasure Island,* by Robert Louis Stevenson. He was so delighted with it that he took to reading books well above his age level.

Reading on his own continued to interest Winston but, when he went to the famous old school at Harrow, he still did poorly in his classes. He refused to learn anything unless he could see some use in it, and he constantly ignored school rules. There is a story that young Churchill once made a bomb the size of a soccer ball to blast the trash out of an abandoned well. At the bottom of the well there was supposed to be a tunnel leading to a haunted house. Winston lit the fuse but nothing happened so he climbed in to study the problem. A Harrow village housewife was horrified to hear a tremendous explosion and see a Harrow boy come flying out of the well. After the alarmed lady got Winston's sooty face cleaned up he said cheerfully, "I expect this will get me the bag."

As it turned out, Winston was not expelled. He actually finished Harrow, and a remarkable man, Robert Somervell, taught him how

Winston at Harrow School in 1889.

to write. "Mr. Somervell," wrote Churchill in *My Early Life*, "was charged with the duty of teaching the stupidest boys the most disregarded thing—namely how to write English. He knew how to do it. He taught it as no one else has ever taught it." Winston had to take the course three times over.

Since his academic achievements were not good enough to get him into Oxford or Cambridge, his family influence won him a place at England's West Point, the Royal Military College at Sandhurst. He had to take the entrance exam three times, but once he got in he did very well. It seemed to Winston that his required studies at Sandhurst were all quite useful. One of the major purposes of Sandhurst in the nineteenth century was to train officers for commanding the troops that maintained law and order in the British Empire. There were almost always small wars, battles, and police actions at the outer edges of the Empire, which included many peoples and territories around the world. To most Englishmen of the time, these battles seemed almost like sports events. In the twentieth century the idea of an empire became seriously questioned. Also, war became more technological. Inventions such as machine guns and land mines meant a soldier did not always have to fight his enemy face to face. Airplanes could drop bombs to destroy whole cities and kill huge numbers of civilians who were not even involved in the actual fighting. Men like Churchill had to change their attitudes. War could no longer be thought of as a game.

In December 1894, Winston graduated from Sandhurst with honors. In January 1895, his father died and in March, Churchill was commissioned as a second lieutenant in the Cavalry. Basic train-

Second Lieutenant Winston Churchill in the dress uniform of the 4th Hussars after graduating from the Royal Military College at Sandhurst.

ing in the riding school was very rough. Soldiers learned to mount and ride horses bareback. They had to jump high bars and learn complicated military maneuvers. The men often fell off their horses. Seven months of painful bruises were the price Winston paid to become an excellent horseback rider. It all seemed worth it later when he became a champion polo player for his regiment.

When the training was over, officers were allowed their first leave. In peacetime they could take five unpaid months per year. Churchill decided to use his first leave to observe Spanish troops putting down a peasant rebellion in Cuba. He also made arrangements with a London newspaper, *The Daily Graphic,* to send regular reports from the scene of action. This was to be his first experience as a journalist.

With a fellow officer, Churchill sailed across the Atlantic to New York City. They stayed with a friend of Winston's American relatives, Bourke Cockran, a wealthy lawyer and liberal politician. As Winston was already planning to go into politics, he had many long conversations with Mr. Cockran. The two became good friends and corresponded for many years afterward. Two of Cockran's principles eventually became woven into Churchill's political philosophy: that countries should trade freely with one another and that governments have an obligation to help the poor.

During his stay in New York, Winston wrote to his mother that he found Americans wonderfully hospitable. To his younger brother, he wrote, "This is a very great country my dear Jack." After their New York stay the two officers took a train to Florida and at Key West they boarded a ship for Havana.

In his autobiography, Winston wrote, "When first in the dim

light of early morning I saw the shores of Cuba . . . I felt as if I sailed with Long John Silver and first gazed on Treasure Island." It turned out to be his first taste of war. On the morning of his twenty-first birthday, Churchill was seated on the ground gnawing on the drumstick of a skinny chicken when there was a burst of rifle fire. The horse behind him was shot and Winston later estimated the bullet had passed only a foot above his head. This was Winston's first experience under fire. Although it did not frighten him, it did make him think a bit. The next evening there was a lot of fighting near camp. When it was finally possible to get some sleep, Winston was glad to notice that the person in the hammock between him and the enemy was a large Spanish officer, "a man of substantial physique; indeed one might almost have called him fat. I have never been prejudiced against fat men."

Back in England Churchill looked around for more action. He applied to join Lord Horatio Kitchener's army in Egypt. Kitchener was preparing for action in the Sudan. Churchill also tried to get a job as a newspaper correspondent in Crete where the Greeks were fighting the Turks. And he tried to use his family influence to join the forces in South Africa where there was a rebellion in Matabeleland. All these schemes failed, and he ended up being sent to India with his regiment.

Airplanes had not yet been invented in 1896. To get to India Churchill's regiment had to travel by steamship. Twelve hundred men boarded the *Britannia* at Southampton, England, and sailed to Gibraltar. Then they steamed the length of the Mediterranean Sea to Port Said, Egypt, and through the Suez Canal. The steel plates of the ship magnified the steaming hot weather of the Red Sea and the

Indian Ocean was frequently rough. "It may be imagined," Winston wrote in *My Early Life*, "how delighted our whole shipful of officers and men were after being cooped up for nearly a month to see the palms and palaces of Bombay . . . across the shining and surf-ribbed waters."

Life for a young officer in India was leisurely and boring. "I vegetate," Winston wrote his mother, but he used the time for education. He read many volumes of history and economics. After six months, Churchill thought he might take a month's leave in England. His mother was incensed. She wrote, "You seem to have no real purpose . . . life means . . . hard work if you mean to succeed."

Winston came home anyway, and while he was there made his first political speech for the Conservative party. He praised the government's Workman's Compensation Bill and went on to describe the function of the British Empire as a "mission bearing peace, civilization and good government to the uttermost ends of the earth." Like most Englishmen of the time, he ignored the fact that a country running an empire is in the business of exploiting less developed nations.

Shortly after this, he learned of trouble on the Indian frontier. That news was, of course, enough to make him cut short his leave and put aside the novel he was writing. When he got back to India he was soon at the scene of fierce battles against Afghan tribes on the northwest border. Churchill enhanced his budding reputation as a writer by sending "frontier letters" to *The Daily Telegraph* in London. After the fighting he published his first book, *The Malakand Field Force.*

Upon his return to England, Churchill learned that Lord Kitchener's expedition was now ready to recapture the Sudan for Egypt. In 1870 the British had begun a conquest of the Sudan on behalf of Egypt, which was then a member of the Empire. In a decade of occupation, they established forts along the Upper Nile and abolished the slave trade. In 1885, Arab tribes killed the British commandant and drove the British out.

Lord Kitchener had more than enough officers and did not want young Churchill in the expedition. That did not discourage Winston. Using his family connections, he managed to wangle a commission in the 21st Lancers headed for Egypt. He also contracted to write a column for *The Morning Post* about the expected military actions. But he still had politics on his mind. On his way up the Nile River, he wrote to his mother to please set up some political rallies for his return. He wrote to a fellow officer that "it would be a very great nuisance to be killed."

Churchill saw extremely hot action in the war in the Sudan. He was very careless about being shot at and took part in the last British cavalry charge in history. Afterward he wrote his second book, *The River War*. In this bestselling account of the campaign in the Sudan, Winston criticized Lord Kitchener for failing to show compassion to the vanquished enemy. After the famous cavalry charge, thousands of wounded Arabs were left on the desert sand to die in the blazing sun. Later Kitchener ordered the destruction of a holy building in the city of Khartoum. Churchill deplored this as an act of vandalism. The young officer was learning to despise the brutality of war.

In the early summer of 1899, Churchill was invited to run for

Parliament as the Conservative candidate for the prosperous working class town of Oldham. The British Parliament consists of two houses. The House of Lords, which meets infrequently and has severely limited political power, is made up of lords and ladies who have either inherited their titles or been awarded them by the King or Queen. Churchill was to run for the politically stronger House of Commons, which is elected by the people. In the last week of the campaign he made eight speeches a day and still lost the election. It was very close but the young candidate was not really disappointed. He was just beginning his career.

In the fall it seemed clear there was going to be serious trouble in the Republic of Transvaal, which today is one of the four provinces of the Republic of South Africa. The Dutch farmers, or Boers, were becoming upset with English entrepreneurs who had come to mine gold and diamonds in the area. Churchill did not intend to miss the action, so he arranged to be a war correspondent for *The Morning Post*. He sailed for Cape Town on the fourteenth of October, and by the time his steamer docked on the thirty-first the Boer War was in progress.

Not long after his arrival, while helping to get an armored train past some derailed cars, Winston was captured by Boers and sent to Pretoria, the capital of the Transvaal. Churchill spent his twenty-fifth birthday in prison. In the middle of December, he escaped and, with no map and no knowledge of the language, started a three-hundred-mile trek through hostile territory. While the Boers posted a reward of twenty-five pounds for Churchill's recapture, dead or alive, he made a lucky contact with some English people.

War correspondent Churchill at the entrance of an Army tent in South Africa in 1899.

A group of Boer soldiers known as Commandos.

They first hid him in a mine shaft and then got him on a freight train bound for Portuguese East Africa. From there he took a steamer down the coast to the port of Durban.

The war had been going badly for the British. When news of Winston's escape reached England, it gave the country a boost in spirits. He continued writing for the *The Morning Post* and took part in the fighting to free Ladysmith, a British town besieged by the Boers. He also got into trouble for being a busybody. In his news articles and in a long letter to a South African paper he called for leniency toward the Boers when the British eventually won the war.

A portrait of Churchill taken in Boston while he was on a lecture tour in the United States in 1900.

Both his newspaper and his commanding officers felt he had no business expressing this opinion in public.

Before leaving for England, Churchill completed a book about his South African adventures called *London to Ladysmith via Pretoria.* When he came home to run for election from Oldham, he was a national hero. The election was close, but this time Churchill won. He was a member of Parliament at the age of twenty-five.

Soon after his election to Parliament, Churchill went on a lecture tour of the United States and Canada. In general, the tour was a great success. Irish-Americans, however, did not like Winston for they had sympathized with the Boers during the recent war. In New York, he was introduced to his first audience by Mark Twain. In Washington, he met President McKinley and Vice-President Theodore Roosevelt. He was in Winnipeg, Manitoba, in Canada on January 22, 1901, when he learned of the death of Queen Victoria.

The meeting of the new Parliament was called for mid-February by King Edward VII. On February 14, 1901, Winston Churchill took his seat in the House of Commons. He would spend the rest of his life as a very visible public figure.

Churchill in London, 1907. Some of his fellow Members of Parliament called him "a young man in a hurry."

CHAPTER III

YOUNG MAN IN A HURRY

LATE IN THE FIRST YEAR of his political career, Churchill read a book which he said nearly made his hair stand on end. *Poverty: A Study of Town Life,* by a Quaker philanthropist named Seebohm Rowntree, described the terrible living conditions of the poor people in the city of York. This may have been the beginning of his concern with his own political party. The Conservative party had also been his father's party, and it was running the British Government in 1901. "I see little glory," wrote Winston, "in an Empire which can rule the waves and is unable to flush its sewers."

One Conservative project that bothered Winston a great deal was the effort to establish tariffs, or taxes, on goods imported from continental Europe. He felt that tariffs would only encourage other nations to create even higher tariffs. The tax barriers between nations could escalate and lead to conflict. Winston thought that free trade among nations would lead them to cooperate with one another. They would then be less likely to attack each other. Winston believed free trade could help insure peace among nations.

Winston's speeches against tariffs annoyed the Oldham Conservative Association. They informed him he would not have their support in the next election. In Great Britain a person may run for Parliament in any district that invites him to be a candidate. Winston accepted an invitation from North-West Manchester to stand for election as a Free-Trade candidate. He was not officially a

Winston speaks to a crowd in Manchester during an election campaign.

member of the Liberal party but, like the Liberals, he wanted to strike a balance between socialism and capitalism.

In a completely capitalistic system, private businesses are free to create whatever economic policy they want regardless of the needs of the people. In a socialistic system the government controls all economic policy. Even though Winston hated socialism as a form of government, he believed both socialism and capitalism had some good things to offer. He felt that the ideal form of government would be to combine the best from each system to create strong economic policy and raise the standard of living for everyone in the country.

Churchill continued to resist the strictly capitalistic policies of the Conservatives. He also opposed the government's total control of Ireland. He spoke against a proposed bill to severely limit Jewish immigration from Russia to England.

On May 31, 1904, Winston entered the House of Commons and sat down with the members of the Liberal party. He had declared his independence from the privileged world of his family. Churchill poured all his energy into criticism of the government and lost some of his old friends. He also gained some new friends, and ignored the political storm he had created by working on a biography of his father. From early childhood Winston had admired his father from afar. Lord Randolph's many human weaknesses were not mentioned in the biography.

In December 1905, the Liberal party won a national election. In British politics, the King or Queen asks the leader of the winning party to form a new government. The new Prime Minister then chooses his cabinet from members of Parliament. These department heads do not give up their seats in the House of Commons when they take office in the Cabinet. Prime Minister Sir Henry Campbell-Bannerman asked Winston to be a junior minister in the new government. As Under-Secretary of State at the Colonial Office, Churchill drafted the final settlement between the Transvaal and Britain, granting self-government to the Transvaal. In all of Britain's colonial affairs, he insisted on justice rather than exploitation.

In domestic policy, Churchill believed that government should take a stronger interest in the welfare of the people it governed. He wanted to establish "minimum standards of life and labor." In April 1908, a new Liberal government gave Churchill an opportunity to initiate some social improvements when it included him in the Cabinet as President of the Board of Trade. According to the Parliamentary rules at that time, however, a politician accepting a Cabinet position had to seek re-election immediately. In the by-election in North-West Manchester, Churchill lost when Catholic voters turned against him. They were upset with him because he had not yet made up his mind to support Home Rule for Ireland, which was then still a part of Great Britain. To remain in the Cabinet, Churchill needed a new constituency right away. The Liberal party identified several by-elections which were coming up. Winston chose Dundee, Scotland. He won comfortably and went on to represent Dundee for the next twenty-four years.

Despite Winston's busy schedule, there was time for romance. In March 1908, he met a young woman named Clementine Hozier at a party. He failed to recall that they had actually been introduced four years earlier. All that summer they corresponded. In August,

Clementine Hozier,
soon to become
Mrs. Winston Churchill,
1908.

Miss Hozier accepted Winston's invitation to visit his family at Blenheim Palace, where he proposed to her. They were married in September and after a honeymoon in Italy they returned to London where Churchill threw himself into social reform. Old-age pensions and unemployment insurance were two of his favorite projects. He also urged steps to prohibit child labor.

Winston and Clementine's first child, a daughter named Diana, was born in July 1909. Churchill felt very loving toward the new baby and wanted to bathe her whenever he had time. People who did not know how warmhearted Winston really was were surprised. Those who saw him only in public found it hard to imagine him as

Clementine, a friend, daughter Diana, and Winston on their way to Buckingham Palace.

a family man. Also, it was unusual in those days for a man to take such an intense interest in household matters.

As early as 1909, five years before World War I broke out, there were a few people on both sides of the English Channel who felt that Germany and England were headed for war. The economic interests of the two countries appeared to be in direct conflict. A few years earlier, Winston had said in the House of Commons, "A European war cannot be anything but a cruel and heartrending struggle." It could only end in "the ruin of the vanquished" and the "exhaustion of the conquerors." Churchill hoped that military strength could still be maintained at a low enough level to leave money in the national budget for what he called "the war against poverty."

On a European tour in September, Winston saw the German Army on maneuvers and was impressed by its great strength, size, and discipline. He reflected on the horrors of war as he had experienced them and, in a letter to Clementine, wrote that despite his training in warfare he had come to see "what vile & wicked folly & barbarism it all is." Back in England in November, he expressed

Winston, second from right, with German officers at German army maneuvers, 1909.

concern over German naval expansion. Nevertheless, his main concerns were still on the social front at home. After the elections of February 1910, Churchill was given the important cabinet post of Home Secretary, thus demonstrating that he had become a major figure in the Liberal party. Among other responsibilities he now had supervision over the British prison system.

Winston campaigned to reduce the number of prisoners. An enormous percentage of the people in the prisons were there for drunkenness. Churchill pointed out that when they were released they tended to celebrate by getting drunk again and so they got sent back to prison. Why not have drunks pay a fine instead of going to jail? They might then have less money to spend on liquor. Many other prisoners were young people locked up for rowdiness and vandalism. Winston noted that university students were often charged with similar crimes but were released on payment of fines. Why not offer working class youths the same choice? For criminals who had to be in prison, Churchill urged that the government find ways to offer them educational opportunities.

In November of 1910 a strike was called by the Welsh coal miners. Rioting and violence spread across Wales and the Army was called in. Churchill was convinced that the arrival of soldiers would only make matters worse. As Home Secretary, Winston could intervene. He ordered the soldiers to be held in reserve and sent two hundred London policemen to restore order. He also offered the strikers a chance to meet with the government. The strikers accepted the offer but the problems in Wales took a long time to settle.

In May 1911, Clementine gave birth to a son, who was named Randolph after Winston's father. "Chumbolly," wrote Clementine, using the new baby's nickname, "grows more darling & handsome every hour, & puts on weight with every meal; so that soon he will be a little round ball of fat."

In the summer of 1911 a dockers' strike began in Liverpool and spread to London. Even though there were negotiations in progress, rioting broke out in Liverpool and violence threatened the London docks. Both Army and police had to be called in, but Churchill still felt sympathy for the workers. He reported to King George V that the dock workers were very poor and "nearly starving."

Then in August there was a railroad strike throughout Great Britain. More troops and police had to be called in to guard trains that hauled food and other essential supplies. Negotiations continued in London, but when peace was made Churchill had become a figure of controversy. Conservative newspapers criticized him and liberal ones praised him.

While the labor crisis was being settled a controversy between Germany and France caught Churchill's attention. He realized, as few others did, that military struggle between the two could result in a disastrous European war. To protect herself from occupation, England would have to side with France. As an island nation England needed a strong navy, but Winston was afraid the ships and officers were not ready.

After studying the situation, Churchill became convinced that reorganization was necessary. He urged Prime Minister Herbert Asquith to appoint him First Lord of the Admiralty so he could be in charge of the Navy. In October 1911, Winston was appointed and immediately threw himself totally into making the Navy prepared for war. He made every detail his business. He visited naval bases to make sure they were well supplied. He studied naval strategy and inspected ships. He started a program to convert the Navy from coal-burning to oil-burning ships. He urged that England establish a Royal Naval Air Force. Over Clementine's objections, he even took flying lessons himself.

The Churchills visit an airfield at Hendon.

A pair of twelve-inch guns on a new British battleship.

Early in 1912, Churchill started to learn as much as he could about German naval planning. He soon concluded that Germany's strength was growing at an alarming rate. In July, he presented Parliament with a plan to increase the number of all kinds of British Navy craft. He also asked that sailors' pay be increased.

During 1913, some members of the Cabinet began to wonder about Churchill's proposed expenditures. Some thought it a poor idea for a Liberal government to be involved in such heavy military spending. Churchill claimed he had prepared a very tight budget and threatened to resign if the Cabinet could not go along with it. Finally he agreed to some minor reductions and his proposed expenditures were accepted by the Cabinet and later by Parliament.

Winston and Clementine at the beach in Kent, summer of 1914.
This was the last holiday before war broke out.

The event that triggered World War I happened on June 18, 1914. Archduke Ferdinand, heir to the throne of Austria-Hungary, was shot to death in the Bosnian city of Sarajevo by a Serbian nationalist. For the rest of the summer, all of Europe watched nervously while Austria demanded retribution and Serbia offered reconciliation. If Austria attacked, because of ethnic ties Russia would side with Serbia and Germany would side with Austria. Because of a previous agreement, France would side with Russia against any country that was its enemy. What would England do?

The British Cabinet was divided. Some, including Churchill, felt that if Germany attacked France, England, which was just across the English Channel, would be in danger and would have to fight to protect herself. Others pointed out that there was no treaty between England and France. These ministers felt that England could safely sit back and watch the European war.

On August 1, Germany declared war on Russia. Russia reminded France of their treaty to help each other in case of war. Before Germany could fight Russia she would have to attack France quickly. She would have to go through Belgium to do this, and Belgium had a treaty with England.

On August 2, Germany demanded the right to pass through Belgium. On August 3, England informed Germany that if the German Army crossed the Belgian border, England would attack. The Germans did not answer but their troops marched on into Belgium. On the night of August 4, Churchill sent a message to all ships and Navy bases: "Commence hostilities against Germany."

The First World War had begun. At the time no one suspected there would ever be a second one, so it was called the Great War.

A cannon called the howitzer was the workhorse of the British Artillery in World War I.

CHAPTER IV

WAR AND POLITICS

CLOUDS OF CONTROVERSY OFTEN SURROUNDED Churchill early in the war. In a democracy, managing a war is like walking the high wire in a circus. Plans and strategies have to be kept secret from the enemy, but the public wants to know what is going on. When people do not understand the full meaning of military events, they become upset with the leaders who plan them. Winston's personal need for action usually made matters worse. He frequently crossed the English Channel to manage military affairs when he might have done better to stay in London and pay attention to politics.

Churchill was on one of these visits on September 22, 1914, when the Germans sank three British ships in the North Sea and fifteen hundred men were lost. Churchill was blamed for the disaster because it was not then public knowledge that he had instructed the ships to stay away from the area. It did not help matters that he was out of the country at the time. And it did not help that on October 3 he was in Antwerp supervising and encouraging the Belgians in the defense of their city. Prime Minister Asquith had approved the trip, but he and other Cabinet ministers were concerned that this non-naval expedition left the Admiralty without strong leadership. Winston was on his way back to London on October 7 when Clementine gave birth to Sarah, their third child. He visited them briefly before going on to report to the Cabinet.

One colleague thought Churchill was a hero and said, "I admire his courage and gallant spirit and genius for war." Another felt that Winston had been much too inclined to take over all operations in Belgium. These mixed opinions were reflected throughout the country and would soon get him into trouble. When Antwerp surrendered on October 10, many people did not realize that Churchill's efforts had helped the city hold out a week longer than anyone thought it could. Nor could they know then that this week gave the Allies the time they needed to reinforce the French ports along the English Channel. Dunkirk and Calais remained in Allied hands throughout the war, thus preventing the chance of a German invasion of England. Nevertheless, the Conservatives, the newspapers, and the general public blamed Churchill for the fall of Antwerp.

Meanwhile, there was more trouble brewing in the Navy Department. The chief of naval operations, known as the First Sea Lord, was Prince Louis of Battenberg. He was a highly respected British admiral who had been born in Germany. Anti-German feeling was so strong in England that Battenberg was forced to resign. Winston wanted to replace him with a former First Sea Lord, the fiery Admiral Sir John Fisher who had retired before the war started. The King opposed the appointment, but Prime Minister

Map of Europe and North Africa showing place names relevant to the life of Winston Churchill.

Asquith persuaded him to change his mind. Churchill got his new Sea Lord.

While this was going on, another naval defeat took place far away off the coast of Chile. The British admiral in command of a squadron had ignored orders to keep all his ships together. A German squadron attacked, killing fifteen hundred men including the admiral. Again, people who did not know about the Admiralty orders blamed Churchill for the disaster.

All through October and November, battles raged around Ypres in Belgium. Every few days, Winston would receive news that another of his friends had been killed on the front. He was worried about his younger brother, Jack, who was at Ypres. The armies were dug into trenches and neither side could advance. Trench warfare seemed to have become endless killing with no progress. It was impossible to cross the enemy's trenches.

In a letter to the Prime Minister, Churchill suggested building some experimental tractors equipped with caterpillar treads. If these were armored with bulletproof steel plates, men could sit inside, firing machine guns and heaving hand grenades. Winston thought such "landships" could cross trenches and move on behind enemy lines. Asquith passed the letter to the War Office, which began detailed study and design. Churchill got other military engineers started on similar experiments and finally, in 1916, landships, now called tanks, appeared at the Battle of the Somme. After the war, Winston wrote, "There never was a person about whom it could be said 'This man invented the tank.'" Churchill had suggested the idea and many other people made it possible.

Prime Minister Asquith, Winston, and three other Cabinet mem-

Soldiers slog through a muddy trench in France.

A British Mark V tank.

bers had formed a War Council to consider all possible ways of opening another front. They thought that if they could defeat one of Germany's allies, Turkey perhaps, the job of defeating Germany would be easier and quicker. In December, Winston had thought about ways to capture the Turkish city of Constantinople, now known as Istanbul. On January 3, Admiral Fisher sent Churchill a plan for attacking Constantinople by sending a naval force through the Dardanelles, the narrowest part of the waterway that connects the Aegean Sea to the Black Sea.

Churchill and his advisors felt that such an attack would be very risky if it was to be only a naval event. It would have a much better chance for success as a combined Army and Navy effort. Lord Kitchener of the War Office, Winston's old commander in the Sudan, said there were no troops to be spared for such an effort. Vice-Admiral S. H. Carden, who would be in command of the campaign, suggested a plan to take Constantinople by naval operations alone with heavy bombardment of the Gallipoli peninsula at the entrance to the Dardanelles. Churchill's office began to work on the details and by the end of January the War Council accepted the Dardanelles plan.

The planning for the campaign was very complex and various officials had differing ideas of what it was supposed to accomplish. Sometimes troops were available, sometimes they were not. Admiral Carden had a much more difficult time than anyone thought he would. The fighting went on into May, when Churchill and Fisher had a series of disagreements which led to Fisher's resignation. The Conservatives, who had been left out of all war planning, raised a loud complaint. They demanded participation in the War Council. They also called for Churchill's resignation. To avoid a Parliamentary crisis, Prime Minister Asquith agreed to form a coalition government which would include both parties in the Cabinet and on the War Council.

Despite the participation of many people in planning and ordering the Dardanelles campaign, the Conservatives believed the lack of success was all Churchill's fault. They wanted him out of the Admiralty and out of the government. He had to resign from the Admiralty. He remained on the War Council, but his advice was generally ignored. Winston sank into a deep depression. He thought

A British battleship firing a broadside.

ANZACS charging. When troops were available for the Dardanelles campaign, soldiers from Australia and New Zealand were among them.

that, at the age of forty, he was a complete failure. He believed his career was over.

Many years later, Clementine would recall that of all the crises she and Winston had lived through, the Dardanelles campaign was the most painful. She had been very worried for him through all the months of horrible slaughter and at the bitter moment of resignation. "I thought he would die of grief," she said. Churchill described his sudden inactivity in his essay on painting. "Like a sea-beast fished up from the depths, or a diver too suddenly hoisted, my veins threatened to burst from the fall in pressure. . . . At a moment when every fibre of my being was inflamed to action, I was forced to remain a spectator of the tragedy, placed cruelly in a front seat."

Fortunately, Churchill discovered a wonderful means of chasing away the clouds of personal gloom. One Sunday he experimented with his young nephew's painting set and decided to buy some oil paints and equipment for himself. He did not know quite where to start, but since the sky was blue that day, he decided to begin there. "Very gingerly I mixed a little blue . . . with a very small brush and . . . made a mark about as big as a bean." It didn't seem like much of a beginning, but just then the wife of the famous painter, Sir John Lavery, arrived. "Painting!" exclaimed Hazel Lavery. "But what are you hesitating about? Let me have a brush—the big one." She splashed the brush into turpentine, hastily mixed blue and white, and slapped "several large fierce strokes of blue on the absolutely cowering canvas." This example was all Winston needed to revive the enthusiastic energy with which he usually greeted new challenges. "The sickly inhibitions rolled away," he wrote later. "I have never felt any awe of a canvas since."

Perhaps because he had wanted to influence so many aspects of the war, Churchill appeared to have more control over it than he actually did. As a result, he became the whipping boy when events went badly for the British. In August the Dardanelles offensive failed. In the press and in public, Winston was given sole blame for the past year's lack of success, including mistakes made after he was forced out of the Admiralty. He was even held responsible for blunders made in the land war over which he had never had any control.

Feeling totally useless in government, Churchill decided to join the fighting. In November, he resigned from the Cabinet and, with the rank of major, was posted to France. Life at the front was very

Lieutenant Colonel Winston Churchill with officers of the Royal Scots Fusilliers.

primitive. The trenches were often muddy, and sometimes infested with rats. To Winston, who always frolicked like a pink porpoise in at least one luxurious hot bath every day, it must have seemed a squalid existence. Nevertheless, he was cheerful about the change. "I did not know what release from care meant," he wrote to Clementine. "I do not ever show anything but a smiling face to the military world," and to the soldiers under his command he said, "If you can't smile, grin."

With characteristic energy, Churchill threw himself into the daily details of his battalion. For six days at a time they were in the front lines. Huddled in filthy trenches, soldiers endured hours of enemy bombardment. Whenever the shelling stopped they would scramble out of the trenches and charge across "no man's land," toward the enemy trenches, in an effort to advance the front line. Territory gained on one day was often lost the next. The casualties were horrendous, especially among the young officers who led the charges. The nations of Europe lost the best of a generation of leaders in World War I.

After a turn at the front, the troops would pull back to rest but only less than a mile from the action and still within range of the German artillery. During these rest periods, Winston did paintings of the blasted landscape around them. A fellow officer described Churchill's intense and irritable concentration and final happiness with one painting. "I have been worried because I couldn't get the shell-hole right," said Winston. "However I did it, it looked like a mountain, but yesterday I discovered that if I put a little bit of white in it, it looked like a hole after all."

By the spring of 1916, Churchill's natural restlessness reap-

A shell-torn village in France.

peared. Politics at home had been preventing him from getting a military promotion and he longed for permission to return to Parliament. But Clementine thought he should remain in France and wait patiently for the right opportunity. They discussed this lovingly in almost daily letters. Finally, in May, unable to stand being left out of governmental affairs, Churchill applied to return to "public duties which have become urgent." Permission was granted.

The failure of the Dardanelles came back to haunt Winston

when he returned. Prime Minister Asquith, in an effort to protect his own reputation, did not want to make all the facts public, and many people continued to blame Churchill for the disaster. As a result, he was not offered a Cabinet position and was forced to remain frustrated in the House of Commons. In December there was a political crisis and David Lloyd George succeeded Asquith as Prime Minister. In July 1917, Lloyd George appointed Churchill Minister of Munitions. The outcry from the Conservatives was furious, but Lloyd George withstood it because he believed firmly in Winston's executive abilities. Churchill showed that Lloyd George's faith in him was well placed by streamlining the department and settling a strike.

There had been a revolution in Russia and in November of 1917 the new Bolshevik, or Communist, government planned to make peace with Germany. This would make it possible for Germany to shift many thousands of troops from the Eastern Front to the West in France. In an effort to do something decisive, Churchill urged the manufacture of tanks on a large scale. But the Germans began an offensive which pushed the British back many miles. Lloyd George sent Winston across the Channel to confer with the French Prime Minister, Georges Clemenceau. The two journeyed to the front and decided that the French and British forces should combine to stop the onslaught.

At the same time the first American troops finally arrived in France. The mere sight of them was a huge boost to morale. They were fresh and eager. They were not in shock from years of trench warfare and they sang songs on the way to the front.

In the early summer of 1918, Churchill and Lloyd George had

to settle more labor strikes at home. By August, Winston felt the tide
had turned in France, mostly thanks to British troops and the tank,
"which British brains have invented and developed." In October the
British stepped up the bombing of German ammunition depots,
airfields, and munitions factories. When Winston went to inspect
the damage, Clementine urged him to return to England to begin
dealing with the problem of what to do for munitions workers who
would become unemployed when the war was over. "I would like
you to be praised as a reconstructive genius," she wrote. "Can't the
men munitions workers build lovely garden cities and pull down
slums . . . & can't the women munitions workers make all the lovely furniture . . . Do come home and arrange all this."

On November 11 the Germans accepted the Allied peace terms,
which had previously been put forward by United States President
Woodrow Wilson. Four days after the Armistice, Winston and
Clementine's fourth child, Marigold, was born. Shortly after that,
Churchill had to face an election in Dundee. His constituents
cheered when he condemned the Bolshevik revolution in Russia,
but they were not so happy when he advocated making a lenient
peace with the German people. Nevertheless, he was returned to
Parliament and Lloyd George put him in charge of the War Office.
Winston now faced the task of bringing nearly four million military
people home and helping them get relocated in peacetime occu-
pations.

There was also another problem for the War Office. The troops
of many nations, including the United States, Great Britain, France,
Japan, and others, were in Russia helping the anti-Bolshevik armies.
There were fourteen thousand British soldiers in Russia and Lloyd

David Lloyd George, who became Prime Minister of England in 1916.

Back in government, Winston speaks at the munitions works at Enfield. Clementine is seated at the end of the table.

*Women
workers in a
munitions
factory.*

George wanted them out. He did not think it was wise for Britain to be involved in another country's civil war. President Wilson thought all foreign troops should pull out of Russia, but Churchill thought it important to maintain a military presence.

The fighting in Russia seesawed back and forth. Sometimes it looked as though the Bolsheviks would triumph. At other times the anti-Bolshevik forces advanced. In mid-October, it looked as though they might win and Churchill decided he would like to go to Russia to help set up the new democratic government. Lloyd George did not seem opposed to this astonishingly busybody idea and Winston was all set to go. But by the end of October the Bolsheviks had had several military successes. The trip was cancelled.

More and more, Churchill became unhappy over being responsible for carrying out policies that had been developed by other people, policies he could not support. He was especially unhappy with his responsibility for sending men and arms to continue the killing and turmoil that had erupted in Ireland. At that time, all of Ireland was governed from London, but the Irish wanted to govern themselves. For some time Churchill had been making speeches in Parliament urging an end to the murder and a beginning of fair discussion. On New Year's Day 1921, Lloyd George asked Winston to take a new Cabinet position, that of Colonial Secretary. As head of the Colonial Office he could preside over the negotiations with the leaders of the Sinn Fein, the Irish party for independence.

One evening at dinner in Churchill's London apartment, one of the Irish leaders, Michael Collins, was grumbling about how the British government had hunted him. "You put a price on my head," he complained. Winston showed him a framed copy of the poster the Boers had put out in 1900 offering a reward for Winston's recapture. "At any rate [yours] was a good price—5,000 pounds. Look at me—25 pounds dead or alive. How would you like that?" Collins thought this was a wonderful joke, and the two men got into much smoother negotiations.

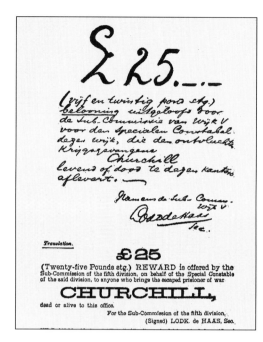

The reward poster issued by the Boers for the recapture of Churchill that Winston showed to the Irish Republican, Michael Collins.

The summer of 1921 was a painful season for the Churchills. Winston's mother died on June 29. In August, after attending the funeral of a family servant, Winston learned that little Marigold had come down with a serious fever at the seashore where the children were on holiday. Winston and Clementine rushed to her bedside and for a week they took turns sitting with her night and day. The best medical treatment did no good and on August 24, Marigold died. Clementine was so upset she cried out "like an animal in mortal pain."

In December 1921 an Irish Treaty was at last signed after many trips between London and Dublin by the Sinn Fein negotiators, Arthur Griffith and Michael Collins. Churchill had hoped that the treaty would be the start of "peace between two races and two islands." The following August, however, Michael Collins was assassinated by members of the Irish Republican Army who disagreed with the treaty. "Tell Winston," he said at the end, "we never could have done anything without him."

In the fall of 1922, Winston bought an old country estate called Chartwell Manor and Clementine gave birth to their fifth child, Mary. Home life seemed bright, but there were storm clouds on the political front. The Conservatives in the old coalition government had come to feel Lloyd George was not the right leader for them. There had to be an election, but three days before Winston was to start his campaign in Dundee he was rushed to the hospital with acute appendicitis. Friends led by Clementine fought the campaign for him but could not overcome the old ghosts of the Great War, the inaccurate memories of Antwerp and the Dardanelles. "In a twinkling of an eye," wrote Winston, in an essay called *Election Memories*, "I found myself without an office, without a seat [in Parliament], without a party, and without an appendix."

Chartwell Manor, the Churchills' country home.

Churchill painting in the south of France.

CHAPTER V

RESTLESS IN EXILE

CHURCHILL FELT IT WAS USELESS to get upset about losing an election. "It only pleases the other side," he wrote. "It is far better to pretend that the matter is of trifling consequence." Privately, however, he saw the situation differently. "Most painful is the grief of your supporters . . . . Men and women who have given weeks of devoted . . . labour, with tears streaming down their cheeks and looking as if the world had come to an end! This is the worst part of all." A week after losing the election in Dundee a friend who had dinner with him said, "Winston was so down in the dumps he could scarcely speak the whole evening."

The gloom did not last long, however. Two weeks after the defeat, Churchill celebrated his forty-eighth birthday and then took Clementine and the children to the south of France for a four-month vacation. He spent the time painting and writing his story of the Great War. The history was to be published in five volumes and would be called *The World Crisis*. When it appeared, it included

Painting done at Avignon in southern France.

many documents about the Dardanelles which had been withheld during the war.

In November 1923, Conservative Prime Minister Stanley Baldwin called a general election. He wanted to reintroduce trade tariffs. Winston had continued to be an advocate of free trade and this was his call to return to politics. The West Leicester Liberal Association invited him to be their candidate for Parliament. Churchill accepted and plunged into a stormy election which he lost. During one of his campaign speeches, a heckler challenged Churchill about the Dardanelles. "What do you know about the Dardanelles?" he replied. "The Dardanelles might have saved millions of lives. . . . I glory in it." But the issue reappeared in another election which Winston lost in March 1924. A Cabinet official remarked, "The Dardanelles pursues Churchill most unfairly . . . if put through with vigour [it] might have shortened the war by a couple of years."

The future of war worried Churchill much more than past wars. This concern led to a new friendship with a prominent physicist, an Oxford University professor named Frederick Lindemann. The two men had almost nothing in common except the fact that their mothers were American. Churchill loved cigars and brandy. Lindemann was a nonsmoker who never touched alcohol. Winston wrote to him while preparing a magazine article, "I have undertaken to write on the future possibilities of war and how frightful it will be for the human race. . . . I have a good many ideas but I should very much like to have another talk with you." Lindemann soon became a close friend and, years later, Churchill's science advisor.

Between Winston's two election defeats the Liberal and Labour members of Parliament had combined to make the leader of the Labour party, Ramsay MacDonald, Prime Minister. The Labour party, originally an association of socialist groups and labor unions, was fairly young as a political party. It was committed to the idea that a socialist government could be achieved by natural political evolution rather than by revolutions like the one that had turned Russia into a communist state in 1917. Winston wanted the Liberal and Conservative parties to join forces against the Labour party. But the Liberal party had lost most of its national support. Winston's daughter, Mary Soames, later wrote, "He now found himself a wanderer in a sort of political 'No Man's Land' between die-hard Conservatism and an enfeebled and disunited Liberal party." There seemed to be nowhere to turn but back where he had come from twenty years before, to the Conservative party. This concerned Clementine who, "in her heart of hearts," wrote Mary Soames, "remained to the end of her days a rather old-fashioned radical."

In June the leader of the Conservative party, Stanley Baldwin, gave up the idea of protective tariffs. This made it easier for Winston to accept the Conservatives' nomination to run for Parliament in the district of Epping in northeast London. In the October election the Conservative party won an enormous national victory and Churchill was back in the House of Commons. Since he was still not truly a member of the Conservative party, Winston did not expect to be offered a position in the Cabinet, but Prime Minister Baldwin wanted him there. Clementine hoped he would be offered the Ministry of Health, because there were so many needs in the social services. Churchill was astonished when Baldwin offered him the post of Chancellor of the Exchequer. Only two years before, Churchill had been out of politics altogether and he lost two more elections after that. This was a triumphant return to public life.

Winston's new position was an important one which his father had held in the previous century. It is similar to the job of Secretary of the Treasury in the United States and includes the responsibility for the national budget. When he took the news to Clementine at their new home in Chartwell, for a while she was convinced he was just teasing her.

Of course, Winston was criticized for switching parties again. In his own defense he wrote an essay called *Consistency in Politics*. In it he quoted the American writer and philosopher Ralph Waldo

*Winston and
Clementine
campaigning in
Epping, 1924.*

*Mrs. Churchill on
her way to hear her
husband's first
budget speech.*

Emerson. "A foolish consistency is the hobgoblin of little minds. . . . Speak what you think now in hard words and to-morrow speak what to-morrow thinks in hard words again, though it contradict everything you said today." Winston's old friend, New York politician Bourke Cockran, was an example of Winston's political philosophy. Cockran was a strong Democrat, but when his party adopted what he thought was a foolish economic policy, he took sides with the Republican party. When the problem was corrected he went back to the Democrats. "This double transference of party loyalties naturally exposed him to much abuse," Winston wrote in an essay called *Personal Contacts*. ". . . never during our acquaintance of twenty years did I detect any inconsistency in the . . . doctrine upon which his views were founded. All his convictions were of one piece." Churchill's convictions were also "of one piece."

The worst crisis for Britain during Winston's five years in the office of Chancellor of the Exchequer was the General Strike of 1927. The social unrest which caused it was only a taste of the bitterness to come in 1929, when worldwide economic collapse brought on the Great Depression. The problem began in the coal mining industry. The mine owners wanted to cut miners' wages. When the miners refused to allow this the owners closed the mines. The Trades Union Congress, which represented all organized labor in Britain, called a general strike in sympathy with the miners. It began on May 3 and went on for nine days, almost crippling the nation. All business and public transportation came to a halt.

A Cabinet committee asked Churchill to plan and edit a Government news-sheet "to relieve the minds of the people." Winston agreed, and established as its editorial theme that the general strike was totally unacceptable, but the problem in the coal industry was still negotiable if the strike could be called off. Within two days, half a million copies of the *British Gazette* had been printed and distributed by volunteers throughout the south of England.

Soon there was violence and looting in city streets. Shortages of basic foods developed quickly. Police had to be called in, reinforced by unarmed and nonuniformed Army troops wearing armbands for identification and carrying nightsticks to quell riots. By May 12 the Trades Union Congress had decided they could no longer support the miners' strike and sent a delegation to 10 Downing Street to inform Prime Minister Baldwin. The general strike was over.

Unarmed, nonuniformed troops wearing police armbands, who helped the police quell riots during the general strike of 1927.

Several days later, Baldwin asked Churchill to take charge of the coal industry negotiations. The owners were still insisting on a cut in wages for the miners. Winston said that if the miners had to take pay cuts the owners had to accept reductions of their profits. He also stated that there was a limit to how much wages could be cut. There had to be a minimum wage level so the miners could earn a reasonable living. Unfortunately, the Cabinet did not support the concept of a minimum wage and Churchill had to withdraw from the negotiations.

In May of 1929 there was a general election. In Epping, Churchill was re-elected, but the Conservative party was swept out of office. Winston was still a Member of Parliament but no longer held an office in the Cabinet. For the next ten years he earned his living writing books and magazine articles at Chartwell.

Churchill's daily schedule was rigid. After breakfast in bed at eight o'clock, he had his first hot bath of the day. Then he would return to bed where he spent the morning reading newspapers, answering letters, and receiving visitors. After lunch with family and friends at one o'clock, he fed his pet swans and goldfish and then worked on paintings in his studio. In the late afternoon he would return to bed for a nap of an hour or more. These siestas enabled Winston to work far into the night when most people were in bed. After his second bath, Churchill dressed for dinner, which often included public figures as guests. The lively table conversation was dominated by Winston. Churchill's real work day did not begin until around eleven P.M. Wearing bathrobe and slippers, he would go to his study and begin dictation to a team of two secretaries. He kept them working feverishly until around three in the morning.

During the 1930s, Churchill's Chartwell work nights produced eleven books and four hundred magazine articles as well as his speeches for the House of Commons.

Some of Winston's fantastic energies were devoted to other projects. He hired a local bricklayer to teach him the trade so he could build a small cottage. He built dams and a swimming pond for the children. And, of course, he continued to paint landscapes both at Chartwell and on vacations in the south of France.

Churchill building a cottage at Chartwell, 1928.

In October 1929, the new Labour government proposed a plan for partial freedom for India. Instead of being a British possession, India would be allowed local self-government but the head of government would continue to be a viceroy appointed by Great Britain. This system was called Dominion Status, and Churchill was strongly opposed to it. It seemed like a risky idea to start dismantling an empire just when it was beginning to look as though Germany wanted to build a new one.

Deep in his heart Winston must have longed to maintain the glory of Empire into which he was born. But in his head he had harsher reasons for opposing Dominion Status. He believed there were "fifty Indias." The Indian subcontinent was made up of a huge collection of provinces, or "rajs." Churchill thought the rajs were not ready for self-government as a single nation. Also, the largest religious group, the Hindus, treated sixty million of the poorest Indians as "Untouchables." Winston was sure that, with Dominion Status, the Hindus would make life even worse for these downtrodden people. He was equally sure that the Hindus and the next largest religious group, the Muslims, would clash, and that both groups would persecute the five million Indian Christians. Churchill could foresee nothing but chaos and bloodshed.

Toward the end of 1929, Jawaharlal Nehru, leader of the Indian National Congress and a fellow graduate of Harrow School, also rejected Dominion Status. His reasons were the opposite of Churchill's. Nehru demanded immediate total independence for India. He called for Indians of every raj and religion to disobey British rule. A very popular spiritual leader called Mahatma Gandhi led a campaign of peaceful civil disobedience. Nehru and Gandhi were thrown into prison.

Eventually, Gandhi was released to attend a Round Table Conference in Delhi to discuss India's future. Nehru remained in jail for most of the next six years. A second Round Table Conference in London in March 1931 resulted in an agreement that gave local government to the Indians but kept Britain in control of military and foreign affairs. The response in India was anti-British riots in Bombay. Hindus fought with Muslims and British officials were murdered. Once any degree of self-rule was suggested, Indians naturally wanted complete independence. As Churchill had warned, "It is no use trying to satisfy a tiger by feeding him with cat's meat." Parliament approved additional partial self-government for India in 1935. Churchill was still concerned but he said to a close friend of

The London Round Table Conference to discuss India's future. Gandhi, wrapped in a white robe, is seated at the table.

Gandhi, "Make it a success and if you do I will advocate your getting very much more."

In December 1931, Winston went on a lecture tour of the United States. It was nearly the end of him. While crossing Fifth Avenue in New York, he was knocked down by a car. He had forgotten that in America traffic moves on the right side of the street, not the left as it does in England. He was wearing a heavy fur-lined overcoat, which may have saved his life. Churchill was very depressed that it took three weeks in New York and two more in the

Churchill leaving a New York hospital after being knocked down by a car on Fifth Avenue, 1931.

Bahamas for him to recover. By the end of January, he was back in New York, where he told a Brooklyn audience of two thousand that the great conflict of the future would be the English-speaking peoples against communism.

Communism, first established in Russia by the Bolsheviks, was becoming popular throughout Europe. To many people the socialistic type of government offered by communism seemed to be the cure for the widespread unemployment and the harsh economic hardship caused by the Great Depression. Twenty-five percent of England's laboring people were out of work and many were attracted to communism. In 1932 it was blamed for workers' marches, rioting, and a mutiny by thirteen thousand sailors protesting pay cuts, but loyalty to the British Empire remained stronger. In Germany, where the economic hardship was at least as harsh as it was in England, resentment over defeat in 1918 was stirring a new national feeling. The steady growth of communism met with competition from a group called the National Socialist Workers' Party. Its leader was a frantic and spellbinding person named Adolph Hitler.

Hitler blamed the Jews and the Bolsheviks for Germany's defeat in the Great War. He expressed his violent hatred of both Jews and Communists in his book, *Mein Kampf,* which he dictated when he was in prison for antigovernment activity. The book also outlined a plan to rule the world. After the worldwide economic collapse of 1929, the National Socialist, or Nazi, party became one of the most popular in Germany. Hitler's paramilitary stormtroopers made it the strongest. In January 1933, amid increasing violence between Nazis and Communists, Hitler became Chancellor of Germany. Later in the year, he withdrew Germany from the League of

Nations, an organization like the United Nations, which had been formed after World War I to safeguard international peace. Germany was rearming in secret.

Even in his last two years at the Exchequer, Winston had been trying to find ways to bolster naval expenditures so that England could at least keep up with the German development of new battleships. When Hitler came to power, Churchill began warning, both in Parliament and in magazine articles, of the danger of

Founder of the Nazi party, Adolf Hitler, early 1930s.

German rearmament. In one article called "Hitler and His Choice," published by *Strand Magazine* in 1935, Winston wrote, "Hitler's triumphant career has been borne onwards . . . by currents of hatred so intense as to sear the souls of those who swim upon them. . . . We have only to read Hitler's book, *Mein Kampf,* to see . . . against whom the anger of rearmed Germany may be turned."

Almost no one wanted to heed the warnings. Pacifism was the mood of the times. Some people even favored total disarmament regardless of what Germany was up to. Winston became the rallying point for the few who were aware of the grim facts. They met frequently at Chartwell. Mary Soames wrote of other occasional visitors, "harassed-looking Germans, Austrians, Poles, and Czechs who, often at great personal risk, came to urge Churchill on in his efforts to awaken the British people to the danger, which yearly loomed larger, before it was too late."

In December 1936 an event which shocked the world briefly diverted Winston's attention. King Edward VIII had fallen in love with an American woman, Wallis Simpson, and wanted to marry her. Mrs. Simpson was divorcing for the second time and English royal custom would not allow the Monarch to marry a divorced person. Nowadays it is hard to imagine that the controversy could have created so much bitterness. There was even a serious debate about it in Parliament. Clementine advised Winston to keep out of it, but he wanted to support the King, who was his personal friend. When he rose to speak in Parliament, he was hooted down. A few days later the King gave up the throne and his younger brother became King George VI. The public criticism flung at Churchill caused him to sink into a depression as deep as the one he suffered after the

Dardanelles crisis. He even thought of selling his beloved Chartwell. "Our children are almost all flown," he wrote to Clementine, "and my life is probably in its closing decade."

That decade became more and more foreboding in Europe. In Spain a civil war broke out and Hitler, along with Benito Mussolini, who had become dictator of Italy ten years before Hitler's rise to power, sent military aid to the would-be dictator of Spain, General Francisco Franco. Some of this aid was delivered in the form of a new horror, bombs dropped on civilians.

In 1938, Germany took over Austria and Hitler demanded that the German-speaking portion of Czechoslovakia, known as the Sudetenland, be turned over to Germany. Just as Churchill and a few others had feared, the threat of a general war in Europe seemed to be growing rapidly. In September, Neville Chamberlain, who had become Prime Minister when Baldwin retired, flew to a conference in the German city of Munich. It was the third time he had met with Hitler in a desperate effort to avoid the terrible slaughter of another war. Chamberlain, Hitler, Mussolini, and Edouard Daladier, Prime Minister of France, talked for twelve hours. Hitler continued to insist that Germany take over the Sudetenland. Chamberlain and Daladier feared this could be the first step in a plan to take all of Czechoslovakia. To keep peace, however, they agreed to Hitler's demand on the condition that plebiscites, or elections, be held for the people of the Sudetenland to show whether they wanted to be governed by Germany or Czechoslovakia. Chamberlain returned to England proclaiming "Peace in our time." German troops occupied the Sudetenland but the plebiscites were never held.

In the House of Commons, Churchill condemned the Munich

Just returned from Munich, Prime Minister Chamberlain broadcasts a message of hope to the British people.

Agreement. "Silent, mournful, abandoned, broken, Czechoslovakia recedes into darkness. She has suffered in every respect by her association with the Western democracies and the League of Nations." Winston was all for friendship with the German people, "But they [the people] have no power," he said. ". . . there can never be friendship between the British democracy and the Nazi power . . . which derives perverted pleasure from persecution . . . and uses with pitiless brutality the threat of murderous force." He ended the speech by describing the Munich Agreement as "the first foretaste of a bitter cup" which would be offered year after year "unless we arise again and take our stand for freedom as in the olden time."

In August of 1939, Hitler and Joseph Stalin, the dictator of Communist Russia, signed an agreement that Germany and Russia would not fight each other. This meant that Hitler would not have to worry about maintaining a battle front to the east when he decided to invade Poland. He probably did not believe Prime Minister Chamberlain's warning that England would go to war to protect Poland.

Winston and Clementine had taken their youngest daughter, Mary, on a vacation in France. There were swimming, tennis, and strawberries, and painting for Winston. Then he had to hurry back to London by plane. Mary and her mother went home by train. As they went through Paris, Mary noticed the train station was crowded with French soldiers.

On September first, the Germans launched their lightning war or "blitzkrieg." Divisions of panzer tanks poured into Poland and the soon-to-be-famous Luftwaffe flew across the border to bomb the cities. In London on September third, Prime Minister Chamberlain went on the radio to tell the British people they were now at war with Germany. Later in the day he called Churchill to the official residence at 10 Downing Street and asked him to take his old office of First Lord of the Admiralty. The signal went out to the British Fleet, "Winston is back."

Winston returning to the Admiralty.

Sheltered in a trench, children watch an air battle over the fields of Kent in the south of England.

CHAPTER VI

THE LION'S ROAR

ALMOST THREE MONTHS AFTER WORLD WAR II began, Winston Churchill turned sixty-five. Many people reaching this age have already finished the best work of their lives and are ready to retire. Churchill's greatest achievement was yet to come.

Winston had only been waiting for Prime Minister Chamberlain to ask him to join the War Cabinet to fly into action. Aside from briskly taking over the Admiralty for the second time in twenty-five years, he quickly became involved in other military matters. He urged the building of more munitions factories and Chamberlain appointed him to a committee for planning and organizing land forces. Many people in England were now realizing that Churchill had been right all the years he had been warning the country about the danger of German rearmament. Whenever he spoke, either in Parliament or on the radio, Britishers began to feel encouraged by his message. He predicted "very rough weather ahead," but he balanced bad news with hope for the future, "The day will come when the joybells will ring again throughout Europe."

The "very rough weather" was even worse than Winston had forecast. Furthermore, it looked as though England and France would have to withstand the storm alone. Other European nations would not join in stopping the Germans from swallowing up the whole continent. Even though Austria, Czechoslovakia, and Poland were already conquered, Denmark, Holland, Norway, and Switzerland did not seem to understand that the same thing could happen to them and remained neutral. Except for Finland, which was then fighting off Russian aggression, Winston scorned the neutral nations. "Each one hopes that if it feeds the crocodile enough, the crocodile will eat him last," he said in a radio broadcast.

At the same time the public and many members of Parliament were beginning to lose confidence in the Conservative government. No one had tried harder to seek peace than Neville Chamberlain. It was almost as though the effort had taken all his energy and left him no strength for fighting a war. In private, Winston often argued with other members of the Cabinet but he felt he had to remain loyal in public. More and more, people were calling for Chamberlain's resignation. Even members of the Conservative party thought that in war the government should be run by a coalition of the Conservative, Labour, and Liberal parties. Many members of all three parties thought Churchill was the only person who could lead the nation.

The crisis got worse suddenly on May 10, 1940, when Germany attacked Belgium, Holland, and France. There were tense discussions in the War Cabinet and with leaders of the Labour party.

Finally, Chamberlain offered his resignation to King George VI. The King then summoned Winston to Buckingham Palace and asked him to form a new government.

Winston Leonard Spencer Churchill had become the new Prime Minister of Great Britain. ". . . as I went to bed at about 3 A.M., I was conscious of a profound sense of relief," Winston wrote in *The Gathering Storm*, the first volume of his history of World War II. "At last I had the authority to give directions over the whole scene. I felt as if I were walking with Destiny, and that all my past life had been but a preparation for this hour and this trial."

Three days later, Churchill told the British people, "I have nothing to offer but blood, toil, tears and sweat." The worst was upon them. Belgium and Holland were lost and German tanks were plunging deep into the heart of France. The Allied forces became isolated on the northern French coast. But the English spirit was not broken. In the last few days of May the stranded troops were miraculously rescued from total disaster. The Navy couldn't carry them all, so a fleet of merchant ships, fishing boats, pleasure yachts, and sailboats ferried 224,318 British soldiers and 111,172 French from the beaches of Dunkirk across the Channel to England. On June 4, Winston told the House of Commons, "We shall fight on the beaches, we shall fight on the landing-grounds, we shall fight in the fields and in the streets, we shall fight in the hills; we shall never surrender."

A week later, Italy declared war on France and England. A week after that the Germans marched into Paris and in another week the French surrendered. Churchill had flown across the Channel in bad weather to persuade them to hang on. A former French pre-

Exhausted British troops being evacuated from the French port of Dunkirk.

mier, Edouard Herriot, later said to Clementine that Winston's "noble words of leadership that day were unavailing. When we heard the French Government's answer and knew that they meant to give up the fight, tears streamed down Mr. Churchill's face."

On June 18, in a speech later broadcast on the radio, Winston told the House of Commons that the Battle of France was over and the Battle of Britain was soon to begin. The full strength of the Nazis was about to be unleashed upon England standing alone. "If we fail," growled Churchill, "then the whole world including the United States . . . will sink into the abyss of a new Dark Age. . . . Let us therefore so bear ourselves that, if the British Empire and its Commonwealth last for a thousand years, men will say, 'This was their finest hour.'"

Germany could invade the country at any time. Winston "drove himself," wrote his daughter Mary, "and he drove others with a flail in his desire to prepare the country for the assault." Someone complained to Clementine and she wrote a concerned letter to Winston. "I was astonished & upset because in all these years I have been accustomed to all those who have worked with & under you, loving you . . . you are not as kind as you used to be." She went on to point out that as Prime Minister he had "terrific power" which had to be used wisely, kindly, and calmly. "Besides you won't get the best results by irascibility & rudeness. . . . Please forgive your loving devoted & watchful, Clemmie," followed by a drawing of a cat.

Perhaps Clementine was not fully aware that Winston had always been rough with people who worked for him. Years before the war he scolded a servant for being rude. The man dared to reply, "But you were rude, too." "Yes," said Churchill, "but I am a great man." Most of the people who ever worked for him simply accepted the fact that he was a most unusual individual. Many of them loved him for it and would work their hearts out for him. Perhaps this was because they knew that Winston demanded more hard work of himself than he did of anyone else.

On July 10, the Luftwaffe began bombing the south coast of England. A tiny British Air Force fought back and the Battle of Britain had begun. "People stood in the summer meadows and watched," wrote Mary Soames, "while overhead desperate aerial combats raged, fought out by a few hundred young men." Churchill himself watched these brave young pilots from a Fighter Command Post in the countryside south of London. A few days later he told the House of Commons, "Never . . . has so much been owed by so many to so few."

Many of the fliers died, but they bought time for London to dig in. Shelters were built and buildings reinforced by the time the "Blitz" began in September. At night, street lights were turned off and windows were tightly shaded so that not a sliver of light could be seen from the air. In spite of the blackout, however, two hundred

Spitfires were the English fighter planes of the Battle of Britain.

Churchill studies plans for the defense of the south coast of England.

German bombers managed to find the darkened city and drop their deadly loads on it for fifty-seven nights running. People got used to the crashes and the sirens and the fires. By the light of the flames, the Cockney working people of London's East End often saw the figure of John G. Winant, the American Ambassador to England. His compassion helped them feel stronger. There were stories of defiance. One woman was hauled out of her wrecked house and stood gasping in the flickering firelight, her hair a mess and blood streaming down her face. "Is yer old man in there?" shouted a rescue worker. "Wot? Me 'usband?" she yelled back. "Nah! The bloody coward's on a destroyer in the Atlantic."

After an air raid.

The map room at the Cabinet War Rooms in the basement of the Government Offices. Heavy timbers overhead support bomb-proofing made of tons of concrete.

Things were equally bad in the Atlantic. In January 1941, President Franklin D. Roosevelt and Churchill had worked out the Lend-Lease Program for Britain to receive many tons of military supplies and equipment from the United States in exchange for the use of military bases in Newfoundland, Bermuda, and the Caribbean. The merchant ships carrying these supplies were being hunted by German submarines in the North Atlantic Ocean. In spite of a convoy system, with naval escort ships to protect the freighters, many of them were being sunk during every crossing. In

March, April, and May a total of 500,000 tons of Allied shipping was sunk by Nazi U-boats and airplanes. Winston found the losses terrifying and said privately, "If it goes on it will be the end of us."

In March, Churchill learned that the Japanese might try to capture the British city of Singapore at the tip of the Malay Peninsula. From there, they could threaten Australia. In April, German troops occupied Yugoslavia. Then they attacked Greece and drove out the British troops. Pro-German Arabs seized power in Iraq and threatened England's oil supply. Egypt was about to fall into Nazi hands and in Libya troops commanded by the German general Erwin Rommel were forcing the British to retreat. In June, Hitler's armies invaded Russia. Churchill had always been opposed to communism, the Russian form of government. He would never change that view. He regarded communism as a threat to democracy, but he thought that nazism was even more dangerous. In a radio broadcast, he explained that it was now necessary to help Russia fight Nazi aggression. "The cause of any Russian fighting for his hearth and home, is the cause of free men and free peoples in every quarter of the globe." Later, Churchill was asked how he could persuade himself to support Russia when he was so adamantly opposed to communism. "If Hitler invaded Hell," he replied, "I would at least make a favorable reference to the Devil in the House of Commons."

The world picture looked terrible, but aid from America was increasing. England's strength was also increasing. Even though the Luftwaffe was still bombing England that July, the British bombed the German cities of Frankfurt and Hanover in an effort to slow the German attack on Russia. Churchill managed to arrange for more help for Russia when he sailed to Newfoundland to meet President

British Lancaster bombers on target.

Roosevelt in August. The Americans agreed to send supplies to Russia and share the escort protection of the convoys in the North Atlantic. They also planned to send bombers to the British in North Africa. Roosevelt and Churchill signed an unofficial document called the Atlantic Charter in which they pledged to support the right of all nations to choose their own form of government, to work toward the improvement of economic and social conditions around the world, and to strive to protect all people from want and fear. The concepts outlined in this agreement later formed the basic principles upon which the United Nations was founded.

In spite of their huge industrial contribution, the Americans were still not actually fighting in the war. Churchill returned to England stating his fear that if the U.S. remained neutral for too much longer, the war would drag on until civilization collapsed. His nightmare was bombed into billowing smoke on December 7, 1941, when the Japanese Air Force attacked Pearl Harbor in Hawaii. The next day the U.S. Congress declared war on Japan. America had been abruptly shoved into the war. Not quite a week later, Winston boarded the battleship *Duke of York* and sailed for Washington, D.C., to meet again with President Roosevelt. Together with the British and American military Chiefs of Staff they coordinated the general strategy of the war. On his way home after Christmas, Churchill spoke to the Canadian Parliament in Ottawa. He recalled that after the fall of France the French General Staff had predicted that Great Britain fighting alone would have its neck wrung like a chicken. "Some chicken!" said Winston. When the Canadians stopped laughing, he added, "Some neck!"

There were still tough battles to come. In February, Japanese troops struggled through the jungles of the Malay Peninsula to attack and capture Singapore, taking sixty-two thousand prisoners. Australian troops fighting in the North African Desert had to be sent back to defend their homeland. British strength was reduced and Rommel's brilliant Afrika Korps pushed them back hundreds of miles. In June, the British were driven out of Tobruk near the Egyptian border. On July 1, Rommel reached El Alamein which is 250 miles inside Egypt. Churchill flew to Cairo to study the situation and decided to put peppery General Bernard Montgomery in charge of the tired British Eighth Army. Monty led a fiery counter-

General Erwin Rommel, commander of the German Afrika Korps.

campaign in late October and nearly destroyed Rommel's army. In November, Churchill made a speech congratulating General Montgomery on his victory. "Now this is not the end," said Winston. "It is not even the beginning of the end. But it is, perhaps, the end of the beginning."

The victory was reinforced by American and British forces landing in the North African ports of Algiers, Casablanca, and Oran. Winston's son, Randolph, was an officer with the British troops. The Americans were commanded by General Dwight D. Eisenhower. Three months later, Eisenhower was made Commander-in-Chief of the Allied Forces in North Africa. He would be an important commander for the rest of the war.

The activity in Africa forced the Germans to divert many tons of supplies intended for the Russian Front. The Russian, or Red, Army was then able to encircle a German Army which had encircled Stalingrad. Churchill pointed out that since the Germans now had to pay more attention to their Eastern Front, the Allies had an excellent opportunity in the west to drive the so-called Axis armies up the Italian peninsula. The name Axis was derived from "Rome-Berlin Axis," a term used in a 1936 agreement between Mussolini and Hitler. General Eisenhower was placed in command of the

German soldiers surrendering to Russians on the Eastern Front.

Allied Forces for this campaign. At this time, Winston also asked his advisors to start making the plans for an Allied invasion of Europe from across the English Channel. In December the British managed to crack the secret code of the German submarines and soon the Germans could no longer dominate the North Atlantic. The tide of Axis aggression had turned.

It was at this time that one of the most horrible activities of nazism became known to the world. Hitler's Third Reich was systematically slaughtering hundreds of thousands of Jews who had been sent to concentration camps. The Allies made a declaration condemning the "cold-blooded extermination" and Churchill said that the murderers had to be brought to trial. He had been aware of persecution of the Jews in Germany as early as 1933. In a September 1937 newspaper article, he had urged Hitler to cease his persecution of Jews and, later, in the House of Commons he had said, "It is a horrible thing that a race of people should be . . . blotted out of the society in which they have been born."

In November 1943, Churchill, Roosevelt, and Stalin met at Teheran in Iran, to begin planning for the conclusion of the war. They decided that Operation Overlord, the cross-channel invasion of Europe, would definitely be in May of 1944. The declaration issued at the end of the conference promised to make a peace which would "banish the scourge of war for many generations." But there was a great deal more war to come. The battles in Italy were harsh. The fight for the town of Cassino lasted five months and resulted in thirteen thousand casualties. The war against the Japanese in the Pacific Ocean moved in agony from one island to another and cost hundreds of thousands of lives. Peace still seemed a long way off.

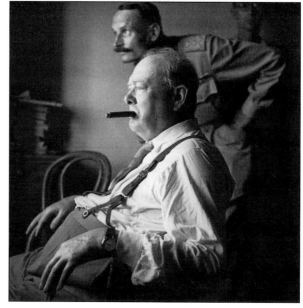

Joseph Stalin, Franklin D. Roosevelt, and Churchill at Teheran, Iran, 1943. Winston's daughter Sarah stands behind Roosevelt. Foreign Secretary Anthony Eden is behind Churchill.

Churchill watches an artillery attack in the Italian hills near Florence.

After the Teheran Conference, Churchill took an eight-and-a-half-hour flight to Tunisia, intending to move on to meet British troops in Italy. He was very sick and exhausted when he landed and it turned out he had pneumonia. Winston was sixty-nine years old. During the war he had sailed across the Atlantic three times. He had made visits to Canada, Greece, and Russia, plus several to North Africa. At the same time he had a full-time job running the government in London. He was tired. "I am completely at the end of my tether," he told General Eisenhower. Doctors were afraid the strain on Winston's heart would kill him. Several family members flew to be with him. "Don't worry," he said to his daughter Sarah, "it doesn't matter if I die now, the plans of victory have been laid, it is only a matter of time." Several days later he told Clementine he was "not strong enough to paint."

By the middle of January 1944, however, Churchill had recovered and he was able to return to England. He immediately threw himself into the supervision of the Italian campaign and the planning for Operation Overlord, which was to be commanded by General Eisenhower. Another problem was developing in Russia where the Red Army was driving the Germans into Poland. Joseph Stalin had promised that the Poles would be free to set up whatever form of government they chose, but actually he had already planned for a Communist government. It looked as though Poland would exchange one tyranny for another. Stalin wanted to dominate Eastern Europe just as the Germans had.

But May was not far off, and Operation Overlord began to demand all of Winston's energy and attention. The staff at the Central War Rooms had fooled Hitler into believing the invasion

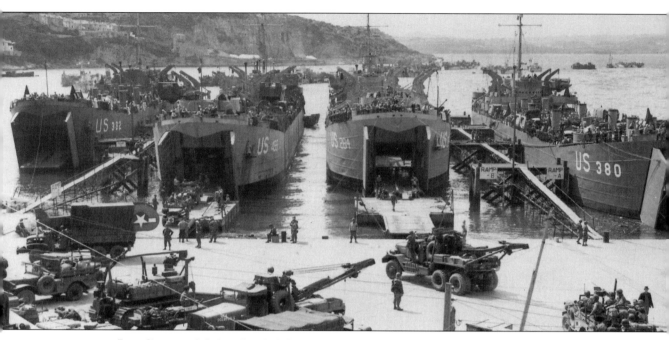

Landing craft being loaded for D-Day at the English port of Brixham.

would take place somewhere near the French city of Calais. The Germans began moving troops and equipment into that area while the Allies made plans for an invasion of the coast of Normandy nearly two hundred miles to the west.

Churchill's daughter Mary was a member of the crew of an anti-aircraft gun. She wrote, "England was splitting at the seams with trained men and every road or free space was filled with equipment and vehicles. . . . In all history there can surely be no other example of such a vast secret being so miraculously preserved."

D-Day was supposed to be June 5, but the weather turned stormy and the invasion had to be postponed for a day. Meanwhile, Allied troops had liberated Rome at last, but people in England hardly noticed. Clementine sent a note to Winston at Supreme Commander Eisenhower's headquarters. "My Darling," she wrote, "I feel so much for you at this agonizing moment—so full of suspense, which prevents one from rejoicing over Rome. . . . Tender love from: Clemmie," followed by a drawing of a cat.

In the early morning darkness of June 6, huge convoys approached the coast of France to drop off thousands of soldiers in landing craft. Within twenty-four hours the Germans were driven off the beaches and by June 12, Churchill himself was crossing the

Royal Marines wade ashore in France on D-Day.

English Channel. By June 18, half a million troops had come ashore, but the Germans were now dug in and the Allied advance fell way behind schedule. To make matters worse the Germans at Calais began launching their recently invented flying bombs toward London.

In early July, the British government was informed of the murder by Nazis of two and a half million Jews in gas chambers at the concentration camp of Auschwitz. ". . . this is probably the greatest and most horrible crime ever committed in the whole history of the world," said Churchill to his Foreign Secretary, Anthony Eden. ". . . all concerned in this crime . . . should be put to death after their association with the murders has been proved."

Inside a concentration camp.

In August 1944, Winston visited Italy to have talks with British generals, Italian politicians, the Greek Prime Minister, and Yugoslav leader Marshal Josip Broz Tito. On the way home he became ill and was rushed straight to the hospital. It was pneumonia again, but he revived quickly. Five days later he sailed with Clementine for Canada on the *Queen Mary*. At Quebec, he met with Roosevelt to discuss the treatment of Germany after the war. While they conferred, news came that American troops had crossed the German border near the ancient city of Aachen. After the conference Winston went with the President to the Roosevelt home at Hyde Park, N.Y., to discuss the use of the atomic bomb, which was expected to be ready in about a year. Then the Churchills sailed home.

On October 7, Winston flew to Moscow to talk with Stalin about postwar peace in Eastern Europe. Today it seems hard to imagine that Churchill actually bargained with Stalin over the future of other nations. He suggested that Great Britain and the United States would have a major interest in Greece. Interest in Yugoslavia and Hungary could be evenly divided and the Soviet Union might have the major interest in Bulgaria. Perhaps Churchill thought this was the only sort of plan Stalin would understand and accept. Certainly, Winston believed Russian Communism was "deadly to the freedom of mankind," and it appeared to be ready to gobble up Eastern Europe. If it could be kept out of Greece, it might be kept out of the Mediterranean countries.

When violence broke out in the streets of Athens in early December, Churchill ordered military support for the Greek government. "The last thing that resembles democracy is mob law," he said to the House of Commons, "with bands of gangsters . . . seizing police stations and . . . endeavoring to introduce a totalitarian regime with an iron hand."

The Christmas season of 1944 seemed special. "The dark war years were drawing to their end like a long and bitter winter," wrote Mary Soames. In Great Britain it seemed reasonable to think it was going to be "the last wartime Christmas. Everywhere families were making their arrangements, despite gaps in the family, despite the blackout and despite rationing."

The fighting in Athens continued and on Christmas Eve, Churchill flew there with Anthony Eden. Clementine was extremely disappointed that Winston would not be with his family on this special Christmas Day, but he was determined to "settle the matter." He met with Archbishop Damaskinos of the Greek Orthodox Church and decided this was the right person to preside at a meeting of all the warring factions, including the Greek Communists. The gathering was almost destroyed by fierce arguments. Winston wanted to step in again and tell them what to do but, fortunately, Eden was able to persuade him that it was time to let the Greeks settle their own affairs.

Toward the end of January 1945, Hitler's armies had been driven back into Germany. It was time for another meeting of the "Big Three" to plan the final campaigns and the end of the war. Churchill, Roosevelt, and Stalin met at Yalta, a Russian city on the Black Sea. In the midst of hopes for peace, Winston was still concerned about human suffering. ". . . my heart is saddened," he wrote to Clementine, "by the tales of the masses of German women and children flying along the roads everywhere . . . before the advancing Armies. . . . The misery of the whole world appalls me

German children watch U.S. soldiers entering their village.

and I fear . . . that new struggles may arise out of those we are suc-
cessfully ending. . . . Your ever-loving husband, W." A few days later
he remarked to Sarah, who had traveled with him to Yalta, "Tonight
the sun goes down on more suffering than ever before in the
world."

Just three weeks after the Yalta Agreement was made it was broken. Many of the free elections the Big Three had planned for the
liberated victims of nazism were prevented by Stalin. In Poland,
priests and teachers were rounded up and sent to labor camps in
the Soviet Union and only Communist nominees were permitted to
run for office. In Rumania the Russian military took over. Eastern

Europeans were being forced to trade the tyranny of Hitler's nazism for the tyranny of Stalin's communism.

In Western Europe, American, British, and Canadian forces continued to advance into Germany. On March 23, Churchill traveled to Germany to visit General Montgomery's headquarters only twenty-five miles west of the line of battle on the Rhine River. The next day, Winston and Monty flew above German positions east of the Rhine and then visited General Eisenhower's headquarters.

Churchill and General Montgomery picnic on the banks of the Rhine.

Events moved rapidly. On April 12, Churchill learned that President Roosevelt had died. On April 17, American troops took Nuremberg and five days later, Russian troops reached Berlin. On April 29, the German armies still left in Italy surrendered. Mussolini was tried and shot by Italians and on May 1, Winston was informed that Hitler had committed suicide in Berlin. On May 4, Admiral Hans Georg von Friedeburg, representing Hitler's successor, Admiral Karl Doenitz, arrived at British headquarters to surrender the

General Montgomery watches a German officer sign a surrender document at British headquarters.

Churchill makes his V for victory sign for a cheering crowd.

German forces in northwest Germany, Holland, and Denmark. Then Doenitz sent General Alfred Jodl to Eisenhower's headquarters in Rheims, France where, on May 7, he signed a document of unconditional surrender. "With this signature," Jodl said, "the German people and the German forces are, for better or worse, delivered into the victor's hands."

May 8 was Victory-in-Europe Day. On the radio, Prime Minister Churchill told the British people, "This is your victory! It is the victory of the cause of freedom in every land. . . . Neither the long years, nor the dangers, nor the fierce attacks of the enemy, have in any way weakened the resolve of the British nation. God bless you all." Winston would always believe the victory belonged to the people. Years after the war he remarked, "I have never accepted what many people have kindly said, namely that I inspired the nation. It was the nation and the race dwelling around the globe that had the lion's heart. I had the luck to be called upon to give the roar."

Collection at Chartwell: Some of the various hats worn by Churchill.

CHAPTER VII

ELDER STATESMAN

CHURCHILL HOPED THE COALITION GOVERNMENT would hold together until the war in the Pacific was over. Clementine hoped that when the Japanese were defeated Winston would retire from public life. Neither hope came true.

The wartime government, which had been hammered together out of the Conservative, Labour, and Liberal parties, was now pulling apart over how Great Britain should be run when the war was finally over. Two weeks after Victory-in-Europe Day, the Labour party decided to withdraw from the Coalition. Churchill offered his resignation as Prime Minister to the King, and an election was set for July 5.

In the course of the war, Winston had become so involved with international issues that he lost touch with domestic issues. As the election approached, he was watching events in Europe. He was very concerned that Soviet Russia's efforts to take over the countries in Eastern Europe would eventually bring on a third World

War. He did not see much difference between Russian communism and British socialism. If communism could stifle free elections just as nazism had, then Churchill feared a Labour government committed to Socialism in England would do the same. This view caused him to make some vicious references to the Labour party in his election speeches. His opponents were angered and his friends were upset.

Listeners to some of the radio broadcasts thought they could hear fatigue in Winston's voice. Churchill himself must have been somewhat aware of the difficulty he was in. Clementine wrote in a letter to her daughter Mary, "He is very low, poor Darling. He thinks he has lost his 'touch' & grieves about it." Clementine also had other worries. Churchill was met by huge cheering mobs of people everywhere he went in the country. But Clementine "had noticed from time to time, as she sat beside him in the open car, that, four or five rows back in the crowds, there were watchful and even hostile faces."

Although the election took place on July 5, the results would not be known for three weeks. It would take that long to collect and count the absentee ballots of the three million men and women in the military services scattered around the world. On July 15, 1945, Churchill arrived in Potsdam near Berlin to attend the final conference of the Big Three. They were going to plan the peace, but it would be difficult. Harry Truman had replaced Franklin Roosevelt as U.S. President. Winston had brought along Deputy Prime Minister Clement Attlee, who was also leader of the Labour party, and would become Prime Minister if the Conservatives lost the election.

Churchill, new U.S. President Harry Truman, and Stalin at the Potsdam Conference, July 1945.

At the Potsdam Conference it was agreed that the Russians would now participate in the war against Japan. Churchill questioned Stalin about violations of the Yalta Agreement which were reported to have taken place in Poland. The Russian leader insisted that the temporary government had done nothing to prevent free elections for the Polish people. Stalin also reassured Churchill that Russia had no intentions of permanently taking over any eastern European countries, formerly occupied by the Nazis, but now under Russian supervision. He guaranteed free elections for all. Later, the world would learn that Stalin's statements were a gross deception. Truman informed Churchill that the tests of the atomic bomb had been successful. On July 24, the two met together with the combined Chiefs of Staff and decided that the bomb would be used within a few weeks. It was hoped that this would shorten the war and save thousands of lives. Later that day, Truman informed Stalin that the United States "had a new weapon of unusual destructive force." Until one of these bombs was dropped on the Japanese city of Hiroshima and another on Nagasaki, no one imagined just how horribly "unusual" and how devastatingly "destructive" this new weapon would be. The new technology would change war and international politics forever.

Good cheer and relief over the conclusion of the war might have been the mood of the Potsdam Conference. Instead, the foundations were being laid for tension between eastern communist nations and the western democracies, which would grow into the forty-year power struggle, or Cold War, between the Soviet Union and the United States. Churchill felt the strain. People traveling with him had noticed he wasn't his usual self. Foreign Secretary Anthony Eden described him as "woolly and verbose." President Truman wrote in a letter to his family in Missouri, "Churchill talks all the time and Stalin just grunts but you know what he means." Five years of long-distance travel and grinding wartime stress had worn Winston down.

On July 25, Churchill and his daughter Mary flew back to London to be present for the election results. Nationally, the Labour Party won in a landslide. Winston was lucky to win re-election in Epping, which had been renamed Woodford. Clementine thought the defeat might be a "blessing in disguise." Winston snapped, "Well, at the moment it's certainly very well disguised." But when someone complained that the people had failed to show thanks for Churchill's hard work he said, "They have had a very hard time." According to constitutional law, Winston could have gone back to Potsdam and resigned after the conference when the new Parliament assembled, but he felt it was important to accept the will of the voters immediately. Clement Attlee flew back to Potsdam as Prime Minister.

On August 14, 1945, Japan surrendered. In Parliament, Attlee paid tribute to Churchill. ". . . In the darkest most dangerous hour of our history this nation found in my Right Honorable friend the man who expressed supremely the courage and determination never to yield. . . . His place in history is secure." Everywhere he went crowds cheered Winston, but at home it was a different story. Clementine wrote to Mary, ". . . in our misery we seem, instead of clinging to each other, to be always having scenes. . . . He is so unhappy & that makes him very difficult."

In September, Winston took a vacation on Lake Como in Italy. He wrote to Clementine, "It has done me no end of good to . . . resume my painting. . . . I feel a great sense of relief. . . . It may all indeed be a 'blessing in disguise'."

In 1946, Winston and Clementine took a trip to the United States. They made many stops, but afterward it turned out that the most important one was in Fulton, Missouri. There, President Truman had arranged for Churchill to make a speech at Westminster College. The title of the speech was "The Sinews of Peace." Its main theme was the importance of the United Nations. Churchill urged that the United States, Great Britain, Canada, and other

English-speaking nations form an alliance to support the UN in maintaining peace.

Early in the speech Winston said that millions of average wage-earners in cottages and apartments around the world "must be shielded from those two giant marauders, war and tyranny." On the subject of international strength he remarked that, "Our supreme task and duty is to guard the homes of the common people from the horrors and miseries of another war." To ward off tyranny, he said, "we must never cease to proclaim in fearless tones the great principles of freedom and the rights of man which are the joint inheritance of the English-speaking world and which through . . .

At Westminster College, in Fulton, Missouri, Churchill gives his "Iron Curtain" speech with President Truman seated nearby.

trial by jury and the English common law find their most famous expression in the American Declaration of Independence."

A quiet dream of prosperity was another theme of the speech. Since he was speaking to an American audience, Churchill thought it fitting to quote his New York friend of years before, Bourke Cockran. "There is enough for all. The earth is a generous mother; she will provide in plentiful abundance food for all her children if they will but cultivate her soil in justice and in peace." Then Winston went on to state that the dreams of peace, prosperity, and free elections were seriously threatened in Europe. "From Stettin in the Baltic to Trieste in the Adriatic, an iron curtain has descended across the Continent." Poland, East Germany, Austria, and other countries once dominated by nazism were now being dominated by Russian communism. Said Churchill, "This is certainly not the Liberated Europe we fought to build up."

Some people scolded him for being an alarmist warmonger. It was the same sort of thing that had happened when Churchill warned about the danger of Hitler. Many people did not want to hear the facts. The title Winston gave the speech was ignored and it became famous as "the Iron Curtain speech." Churchill meant the warning to be a strong part of his message. When he wrote it, Soviet Russia had already established Communist governments in the nations of Eastern Europe; Churchill did not create them. No one seemed to pay much attention to the other part of the speech, the eternal hope of peace and human rights.

Back in Great Britain, Winston launched into writing his six-volume history of World War II. He often sat in the House of Commons and sometimes made speeches. But his main work was now at

Churchill painting in 1946.

Chartwell. Here he worked on the grounds, played with his grand-children, and continued his writing. He also made a number of painting expeditions to Italy and the south of France. Ever since he had discovered oil paints, Winston had labored to make each new canvas better than the last one. Now he was turning out some of his best paintings.

During the next few years the Labour government gradually lost support. In October 1951, the Conservatives won a narrow victory in a national election. At the age of seventy-seven, Winston Churchill was once more Prime Minister. The experience was very different from the war years. Churchill no longer felt he had to be involved in every tiny detail of government. His Cabinet was a capa-

Campaigning to be Prime Minister again, Churchill visits his constituency in Woodford during the 1950 election.

ble team of very remarkable people, including Anthony Eden. Winston felt safe delegating responsibilities to them and focusing his energy on developing strategy, especially in foreign affairs.

In early 1952, Churchill went to Washington to confer with President Truman and the U.S. Cabinet about international issues. They discussed fighting in Korea, problems in the Middle East, difficulties with the Soviet Union, and the need for an Anglo-American alliance. After these meetings, Winston went to Canada where, at a banquet in Ottawa, he gave a speech about ways to prevent another war. Then he took a train back to Washington to address the U.S.

Congress on the same subject. He longed for an alliance of "the governments of the world, not to dominate it . . . but to save it."

Shortly after Winston returned to England, King George VI died. In a radio broadcast the following day, Churchill paid homage to the King and looked forward to the reign of Queen Elizabeth II. But Winston's own health was not good. During the war, Clementine had thought he should leave government as soon as it was over. Now many others thought it was certainly time for him to retire. Some members of the Conservative party, including a few members of the Cabinet, agreed.

In January of 1953, Churchill sailed to New York to visit his old wartime colleague Dwight D. Eisenhower, who was about to be inaugurated as President. Winston's dream of a free and united Europe was his reason for the visit. With Eisenhower he discussed possibilities for a meeting with Stalin. Then Winston went on to Washington for a final visit with Truman. It looked as though Winston would never resign.

In March, after Churchill returned to England, Stalin's death was announced. In April, Winston accepted the Queen's request that he become a Knight of the Garter. Membership in this order is awarded only by the Monarch and it is one of the oldest honors in England. Churchill was now Sir Winston. In May, he renewed his efforts to meet with Russian officials. A preliminary conference of the United States, Great Britain, and France was finally arranged. It was to take place in Bermuda a few weeks after the Coronation of Queen Elizabeth on June 2. But on June 23 Winston had a stroke. His doctor thought he might not live more than a few days longer. The Bermuda meeting was postponed.

In Southampton, Churchill reports on his meeting with U.S. President Eisenhower. Anthony Eden waits in the background.

The nature of the Prime Minister's illness was not announced to the public, but Clementine and Churchill's doctors were sure he could not continue. He would have to resign now. Instead, Winston surprised everyone by making an astonishing recovery. On October 16 he was delighted to learn he had been awarded the Nobel Prize for Literature. On October 20 he made a visit to the House of Commons. His first speech to Parliament after the stroke was made on November 3 and a month later he was in Bermuda for the postponed conference. Foreign Secretary Eden was supposed to succeed Churchill as leader of the Conservative party and as Prime Minister.

Eden was beginning to wonder if he would ever have the chance.

In June of 1954, Eden sent a letter to Churchill suggesting he resign after an upcoming conference with Eisenhower about the peaceful uses of atomic energy. Winston refused. Later he told Eden he would hand the government over in September after an August visit to Moscow, but the Cabinet opposed the trip and forced Churchill to cancel it. Many people were sure he would announce his resignation during the tumultuous celebration of his eightieth birthday, but Winston said nothing about it. In December, he said he would resign after the election scheduled for November 1955. The Cabinet thought waiting that long would weaken the Conservative party's chance of success. On March 8 Winston informed Eden that he planned to retire on April 5. A few days later he withdrew the offer.

The constantly shifting tensions of the Cold War had continued between the Western Allies and the Communist countries of Eastern Europe since the end of World War II. Churchill feared the possible outbreak of a terrible hot war in which each side might use nuclear weapons. He believed his experience put him in an especially strong position to help plan top-level meetings to reduce the tensions. In March, Winston was informed that President Eisenhower was not ready to meet with the Russians. On the evening of March 30, Churchill invited Eden and another member of the Cabinet to 10 Downing Street. When they were seated, Winston said, "I am going and Anthony will succeed me. We can discuss details later." That was the end of the meeting.

Queen Elizabeth and her husband, the Duke of Edinburgh, attended a formal dinner party at 10 Downing Street on the evening of April 4. Winston offered a toast to the Queen's health in which he remembered drinking the same toast long ago for "Your Majesty's great-great-grandmother." The following afternoon, Winston went to Buckingham Palace to offer his resignation officially to the Queen. The day after that the Churchills hosted a tea party to honor the secretaries, telephone operators, drivers, and other members of the staff of 10 Downing Street.

A week after he resigned, Winston and Clementine went on a vacation to Italy. Until a year before he died in 1965, he continued

After his retirement dinner, Sir Winston holds the limousine door for Queen Elizabeth.

as a Member of Parliament for Woodford. He also worked on his four-volume *History of the English-Speaking Peoples* and, of course, his beloved paintings. Science also held his attention, as it had since he first met Professor Lindemann. Once, in a speech at Massachusetts Institute of Technology, he had expressed concern that England had no university-level schools of science and engineering. Now he hoped to do something about the problem. With a lot of help from American business and the Ford Foundation he established a new college for science and technology at Cambridge University. In October 1959, Winston helped plant a tree at the ceremony that marked the founding of Churchill College.

As if the prestigious Nobel Prize for Literature had not been honor enough, Winston continued to receive numerous others. In Paris, on November 16, 1958, General Charles de Gaulle decorated him with the Croix de la Liberation, the highest honor for service to the Free French Forces in World War II. Another award, one which no one else has ever received, was made on April 9, 1963, by U.S. President John F. Kennedy. Sir Winston Churchill was made an honorary citizen of the United States. In making the announcement, Kennedy said of Churchill, "In the dark days and darker nights when England stood alone . . . he mobilized the English language and sent it into battle."

Winston had broken his hip the previous summer and his continued frailty made travel to the United States to receive the award out of the question. Randolph, accompanied by his son Winston II, went to Washington to accept the award for his father. Soon afterward, Churchill sent a letter to his Woodford constituency informing them he would not run in the next general election.

Churchill was unable to go to Washington when President John F. Kennedy awarded him honorary U.S. citizenship. Winston's son, Randolph, accepted the honor for him. Randolph stands on the President's left and Churchill's grandson, Winston, stands behind the President, next to Jacqueline Kennedy.

Early in January of 1965, Winston had a stroke. He slipped in and out of consciousness for the next two weeks and died on January 24 at the age of ninety. On January 30, England held an elaborate state funeral. It was full of the ceremony at which the British excel. It expressed the respect and gratitude of a nation for the services of a favorite subject. Few other statesmen in English history have been buried with so much honor. The music included a nod toward Winston's fond dream of Anglo-American solidarity with the strains of a famous old song of the American Civil War, "Battle Hymn of the Republic."

Churchill's coffin is carried to the boat that will take it up the Thames River to be buried at Bladon Church near Blenheim Palace.

In the middle decades of the twentieth century, when strong-armed dictators denied people free elections, Winston Churchill spoke up valiantly for human rights. He believed people must be free to choose their own governments. He defended this right with ringing words. Churchill knew how to use words as an artist uses colors. He also loved colors and longed to use them as brilliantly as he used words. "When I get to heaven," he said, "I mean to spend a considerable portion of my first million years in painting, and so get to the bottom of the subject. . . . I expect orange and vermilion will be the darkest, dullest colours . . . and beyond them will be a whole range of wonderful new colours which will delight the celestial eye."

Churchill's studio at Chartwell.

Churchill gives sailors his famous V-for-victory sign as he disembarks from the Queen Mary, 1943.

WINSTON'S WIT

Churchill was famous for his clever use of words. In debates with his fellow members of Parliament, in his writing, in private conversations, or in public interviews he was a master of brisk and witty comments.

Winston once described one of his political opponents as "a very modest man. But then he has much to be modest about."

◆

Of a well-known member of the Labour Party Churchill said, "He has, more than any other man, the gift of compressing the largest amount of words into the smallest amount of thought."

◆

"If you cannot read all your books . . . arrange them on your own plan so that if you do not know what is in them, you at least know where they are. Let them be your friends; let them at any rate be your acquaintances."

A lady member of Parliament who was annoyed with Winston said to him, "If you were my husband, I'd put poison in your coffee." Churchill replied, "If you were my wife I'd drink it."

◆

Of a rather dull member of Parliament Winston remarked, "The worst that can be said about him is that he runs the risk of being most humorous when he wishes to be most serious."

◆

"Some men change their party for the sake of their principles, others their principles for the sake of their party."

◆

When he left the Liberal Party to rejoin the Conservatives Winston remarked, "Anyone can rat, but it takes a certain amount of ingenuity to re-rat."

◆

To a political opponent he once said, "I should think it hardly possible to state the opposite of the truth with more precision."

◆

A member of Parliament was giving a long and boring speech when he noticed that Churchill's eyes were closed. "Must you fall asleep while I am speaking?" the man asked. "No," replied Winston with his eyes still closed. "It's purely voluntary."

◆

At the end of his term as Chancellor of the Exchequer, Churchill joked, "Everybody said I was the worst Chancellor of the Exchequer that ever was. I am now inclined to agree with them,"

◆

"During my life I have often had to eat my own words and I have found them a wholesome diet."

An American feminist asked Churchill what he thought the role of women should be in the future. He replied, "The same, I trust, as it has been since the days of Adam and Eve."

◆

When he was asked if he had had trouble sleeping during the war Churchill replied, "Oh no, I just put my head on the pillow, said damn everybody and went off."

◆

"What most people call bad judgment is judgment which is different from theirs at a particular moment."

◆

"I am sure that the mistakes of that time will not be repeated. We shall make another set of mistakes."

◆

"In war you don't have to be nice, you only have to be right."

◆

"It is very much better, sometimes, to have a panic feeling beforehand and then be quite calm when things happen, than to be extremely calm beforehand and go into a panic when things happen."

◆

When he was quite old someone asked Churchill if he was afraid of death. He answered, "I am ready to meet my Maker. Whether my Maker is prepared for the great ordeal of meeting me is another matter."

◆

"A young man cannot expect to get very far in life without getting some good smacks in the eye."

◆

"There is a great deal of difference between the tired man who wants a book to read and the alert man who wants to read a book."

◆

"A fanatic is one who can't change his mind and won't change the subject."

◆

"The inherent vice of Capitalism is the unequal sharing of blessings. The inherent virtue of Socialism is the equal sharing of miseries."

◆

"There is not one single social or economic principle or concept in the philosophy of the Russian Bolshevik which has not been realized, carried into action, and enshrined in immutable laws a million years ago by the white ant."

◆

At Yalta President Roosevelt suggested limiting the conference to five or six days and Churchill grumbled, "I don't see any way of realizing our hopes of a world organization in six days. Even the Almighty took seven."

◆

When President Roosevelt barged into a guest room at the White House and was embarrassed to find Winston still naked from his bath, Churchill said graciously, "Do come in Mr. President. The Prime Minister of Great Britain has nothing to hide from the President of the United States."

◆

Invited to make a speech to the U.S. Congress in 1941 Winston mused, "I cannot help reflecting that if my father had been American and my mother British, instead of the other way round, I might have got here on my own."

When asked why he painted only landscapes and never portraits he answered, "Because a tree can't complain that I haven't caught its likeness."

◆

Explaining how he felt about colors Winston said, "I rejoice with the brilliant ones and am genuinely sorry for the poor browns."

BIBLIOGRAPHY

WORKS RELATING TO WINSTON S. CHURCHILL

Adler, Bill. *The Churchill Wit.* New York: Coward-McCann, 1965.

Blake, Robert, and William Roger Louis, eds. *Churchill.* New York: W. W. Norton & Co., 1993.

Broad, Lewis. *Winston Churchill, Architect of Victory and of Peace.* London: Hutchinson & Co., 1956.

Charmley, John. *Churchill: The End of Glory.* New York: Harcourt Brace and Company, 1993.

Churchill, Randolph S., and Helmut Gernsheim, eds. *Churchill: His Life in Photographs.* New York: Rinehart and Company, 1955.

Churchill, Sarah. *A Thread in the Tapestry.* New York: Dodd, Mead & Company, 1967.

Gilbert, Martin. *Churchill: A Life.* New York: Henry Holt, 1991.

Hough, Richard. *Winston and Clementine.* New York: Bantam Books, 1991.

Ingram, Bruce, ed. *An Eightieth Year Tribute to Winston Churchill.* London: *The London Illustrated News,* 1954.

Lockhart, J. G. *Winston Churchill.* London: Gerald Duckworth & Co., 1951.

Manchester, William. *The Last Lion, Winston Spencer Churchill, Alone, 1932-1940.* Boston: Little Brown and Company, 1988.

Miller, Harry Tatlock, and Loudon Sainthill. *Churchill, The Walk with Destiny.* London: Hutchinson & Co., 1959.

The Observer. Churchill by His Contemporaries. London: Hodder and Stoughton, 1965.

Roberts, Brian. *Churchills in Africa.* New York: Taplinger Publishing, 1970.

Soames, Mary. *Churchill: His Life as a Painter.* Boston: Houghton Mifflin, 1990.

———. *Clementine Churchill: The Biography of a Marriage.* Boston: Houghton Mifflin, 1979.

Sykes, Adam, and Iain Sproat. *The Wit of Sir Winston.* London: Leslie Frewin, 1965.

Taylor, Robert Lewis. *Winston Churchill, an Informal Study of Greatness.* New York: Doubleday & Company, 1952.

The Times *of London,* foreword by Lord Saffron Butler. *The Churchill Years, 1874-1965.* New York: The Viking Press, 1965.

WORKS BY WINSTON S. CHURCHILL

An Address Delivered in Washington on December 26th, 1941 Before the Members of the Senate & of the House of Representatives of the United States. Stamford, Connecticut: Overbrook Press, 1942.

London to Ladysmith via Pretoria. New York: Longmans Green and Company, 1900.

My Early Life: A Roving Commission. London: Odhams Press, 1949.

Painting as a Pastime. New York: Cornerstone Library, 1965.

"Prime Minister" and "Their Finest Hour." In *Into Battle,* compiled by Randolph S. Churchill. London: Cassell and Company, 1941.

Savrola. New York: Random House, 1956.

"The Sinews of Peace." In *The Sinews of Peace, Post-War Speeches by Winston S. Churchill,* edited by Randolph S. Churchill. Boston: Houghton Mifflin Company, 1949.

The Second World War: The Gathering Storm. Boston: Houghton Mifflin Company, 1948.

Step by Step: 1936-1939. London: Odhams Press,1949.

Thoughts and Adventures. London: Odhams Press, 1949.

The World Crisis. New York: Charles Scribner's Sons, 1931.

ACKNOWLEDGMENTS

I have to imagine that my reticent British uncle, John Dunn, might have regarded Winston Churchill as a bit of a buccaneer. Nevertheless, both men were quintessentially British and I am grateful to Uncle John for being "ever-so." I am also grateful to my parents, Frank and Frances Severance, for frequently adding rare and interesting volumes to the collection of Churchill books which I began in London in 1955.

I am indebted to Russell Freedman for giving me the first glimmer of an idea for a book on Churchill during the SCBWI conference at Hofstra University in April, 1993. I am delighted that, five months later, Dorothy Briley of Clarion Books accepted the proposal for the book. Many others have helped along the way. Winston Churchill's youngest daughter, Lady Soames, offered advice and encouragement. Barbara and Kenneth Prideaux-Brune insisted on visits to Blenheim Palace, Winston's birthplace, and St. Martin's Church, Bladon, his final resting place. For assistance with photographs, I am grateful to Paul Kemp of the Imperial War Museum, London; Alan Kucia of the Churchill Archives, Cambridge; Elaine Hart of the *Illustrated London News;* Barbara Natanson of the U.S. Library of Congress; and especially Michael Shulman of Archive Photos, New York.

Most importantly, I am indebted to my wife Sylvia Frezzolini Severance and her assistant Rosemary Buonocore for making it look like a real book.

John B. Severance

PICTURE CREDITS

INDEX